THE NEW DEMOCRACY IN FOREIGN POLICY MAKING

"The President is the sole organ of the nation in its external affairs."

—John Marshall in the House of Representatives (1800)

"The President alone has the power to speak or listen as a representative of the nation."

—Justice Sutherland for the Supreme Court in
United States v. *Curtiss-Wright* (1936)

THE NEW DEMOCRACY
IN FOREIGN POLICY
MAKING

B Y

Norman L. Hill

UNIVERSITY OF NEBRASKA PRESS · LINCOLN

International Standard Book Number 0–8032–0757–3

Library of Congress Catalog Card Number 76–110393

Manufactured in the United States of America

E
840
H48

Contents

Preface

DEMOCRATIC PROCESSES lend themselves awkwardly to the conduct of foreign relations. This has been pointed up by students of government, and it has been demonstrated all too often by American democracy, especially in the last half century, during which the responsibilities of great power have grown heavier and heavier. American blundering in Vietnam is a sobering example of democratic policy at its worst, as both doves and hawks would admit, albeit for different reasons. The usual faults of democracy in foreign policy making have been aggravated by our separation-of-powers structure and by the extremism of today's democracy. Together they have decentralized policy making and turned it into a three-cornered contest of the president, the people, and the Congress (especially the Senate). Pulling in different directions, they tear crucial policies apart.

My contention is that the primacy of the president must be restored. Unlike many Americans, I do not fear strong leadership by a chief executive elected by and responsible to the people, nor do I believe it incompatible with democracy; to the contrary, it is democracy at its best. A democracy that is self-defeating is one prejudiced against the utilization of the best know-how available in government, found as a rule in its own elected president. Serious as it is, democracy's malady can be cured.

PREFACE

Democracy's foreign policy has had a special interest for me ever since I conducted several graduate seminars on the subject at the University of Nebraska a few years ago. Recent unsuccessful ventures of the United States in its policy making have heightened that interest and transformed, for me, a subject of academic interest into the most vital and practical problem facing American democracy.

The libraries of the University of Nebraska and Berea College have been most accommodating to me in providing books and journals. I acknowledge, too, the counsel of Assistant Chancellor Lynn Eley of the University of Wisconsin at Milwaukee, who read the manuscript and made helpful suggestions.

NORMAN L. HILL

THE NEW DEMOCRACY IN FOREIGN POLICY MAKING

1. The New Democracy

A CENTURY AND A HALF AGO "democracy" was a fearsome word and its exponents were considered irresponsible radicals. But as Lord Bryce, one-time British ambassador to the United States, noted in 1921, it had by his time come to evoke not "dislike or fear" but "praise." Since he wrote, "democracy" has accumulated even greater prestige, so that T. S. Eliot could say that to our generation it has become "sanctified." Attacks by Fascists and Nazis upon democracy served to magnify its virtues rather than to dim them. So glamorous has the principle of popular government become that dictators have found it convenient to label the governments which they head "democracies," apparently to delude people at home and abroad into believing that the idealism which the word stands for has become a reality. Mainland China and the Russian satellites are "democratic republics," and Sukarno's Indonesia was a "guided democracy."

Our forefathers who wrote the Constitution at Philadelphia in 1787 were among the many men of their day who were skeptical of the people in government. For the democratic fervor of the Revolutionary years they had no use; it implied more confidence in the people than they had. They stood for a "Republic," as the *Federalist* explained, in which the governing power would be, not in the people themselves, but in representatives

1

chosen by them; and by "the people" they meant that minority of adult males who could meet the rigid property and religious qualifications for voting then maintained by the thirteen states. "It may well be," the authors of the *Federalist* wrote, "that the public voice, pronounced by the representatives of the people, will be more consonant with the public good than if pronounced by the people themselves." So dubious were the men of 1787 of the people's political ability that they did not provide for the direct popular election either of the president or of senators. Instead, for the president they created an electoral college whose members would be selected in each state as its legislature might prescribe; the small size and superior quality of this body would, so they reasoned, provide the nation with more able executives than the people would be likely to elect. Senators were to be chosen by the legislatures of the several states rather than by the people, again to bring to bear the wisdom of a select group.

Since 1787, as democracy has proved itself and gained its present high rating, Americans have gradually enlarged the list of demands which they believe it makes on the political and economic life of the nation. Never has there been a consensus in this country or elsewhere on exactly what those demands are or what they should be, for "democracy" is too elastic a word to be pinned down in its meaning or implications. Until the Civil War settled the issue, slavery was deemed by millions of Americans to be consistent with democracy. Before the Seventeenth Amendment to the Constitution was advocated (and adopted in 1913), there was little objection voiced by ardent democrats to the indirect election of senators by the state legislatures. It took the efforts of Susan B. Anthony and the suffragettes to convince Americans that in a sound democracy women must have the right to vote. Now the idea is spreading that our democracy would be more perfect if young people from eighteen to twenty-one years of age were brought into the electorate. Recently, too, American democracy has been emphasizing political and civil rights for black people. It has also been stressing the needs of the poor and disadvantaged so that their share in the nation's prosperity and opportunities will be equitable. These principles and programs encountered opposition as they were slowly woven into the fabric of the new democracy of today, but few there are who would separate them out, even were it possible to do so.

Probably the most hazardous, although the least opposed, innovation of the new democracy is the enlarged role in decision making which the people have been demanding and actually winning at the expense of the authority of their government. Implicit in this movement seems to be a discontent with representative democracy, wherein the people turn over to a government selected by them at the polls the burden of decision making, and a demand for a more direct form of democracy in which they dominate policies of all kinds, domestic and foreign. No suggestion has been made that the president or Congress be eliminated from the structure of government; the idea is rather that the organs of government become automatons managed by the people, or at least those people who most effectively assert their wishes. A national meeting of all citizens, analogous to the New England town meetings and the Athenian assembly of ancient Greece, might have a strong appeal if it could be made practicable for so large a country; because of its impracticability, other means have been found for promoting the people from the back seat of policy making to the driver's seat, while at the same time relegating government officials to the rear. The initiative and referendum, which became quite general in the states and cities some six or seven decades ago, was the first major advance of the people at the expense of their constituted government in decision making.

This urge to be their own government is at the heart of the new democracy which has come to hold the imagination of Americans. In the past few years, as the urge has mounted, the term "participatory democracy" has come into vogue. No authoritative definition of the term has been made, but usage suggests that it would legitimize activity of any kind, even civil disobedience, by any group or individual, intended to affect decision making on any subject within the purview of government. Its procedures have been employed to promote a new policy, to destroy a present policy, and even to undermine the "establishment." It has been most conspicuous in the field of foreign policy and related subjects—Vietnam, the draft, and nuclear weapons—but it has also been aimed at the men who make policies, Secretary of State Rusk and Presidents Johnson and Nixon, and applied in the areas of civil rights and college administration. Its methods rely largely on public demonstrations. In his recent *Memoirs*, Arthur Krock called the concept "mass democracy" and feared that it would in time reduce the United States to a second-class power.

The most profound of all problems of political philosophy has always been the delimitation of the area in which the people shall carry on as against that in which their government shall function. Plato, Aristotle, Rousseau, Locke, and scores of others have grappled with the question and come up with a variety of answers. In practice, absolute monarchies, dictatorships, and authoritarian regimes (Fascist and Communist) have recognized no area in which the people have an inherent claim to authority, and have therefore left only rebellion as a means of popular action. Democracy, as we understand it in the West, extends to the people a central position; it is government "of the people, by the people, and for the people," as Lincoln said, but it does not prescribe precisely *how* or *at what points* the popular will shall prevail. In this country we have recently been stretching the meaning of "democracy" from a fairly tenable balance between people and government to extreme domination by the people. We have done it, not by amending the Constitution, but by subjecting the government to such measures of intimidation and hostility as to render it submissive, at times paralyzed. Even

2. The Problem

CRITICS OF DEMOCRACY, including its friends, have traditionally been more skeptical of its virtues in foreign affairs than in domestic. Alexis de Tocqueville, in his *Democracy in America* (1835), was struck by its internal benefits, noting that it "is favorable to the increase of the internal resources of the state . . . ; it promotes the growth of public spirit, and fortifies the respect which is maintained for individuals in all classes of society." But he had nothing good to say for it in foreign affairs, arguing that "foreign policies demand scarcely any of those qualities which a democracy possesses; and they require, on the contrary, the perfect use of almost all of those faculties in which it is deficient." The people's lack of patience, their aversion to details, their emotionalism, and their inability to plan or act in secret disqualified them, so he believed, from large-scale participation in foreign affairs. Lord Bryce summarized the position of critics when he said, "Statesmen, political philosophers, and historians have been wont to regard the conduct of foreign relations as the reproach of democracy." Recently Walter Lippmann pointed out in *The Public Philosophy* that the reluctance of the people to go along with policy changes deemed necessary by the government makes it difficult to "prepare properly for war or to make peace." These observations of wise men, whether overpessimistic or not, at least serve the purpose of pointing up democracy's congenital weaknesses.

Foreign affairs are always more "foreign" to the people than domestic affairs. The contacts of citizens with their government at home are legion. They pay taxes—municipal, state, and national—in government offices or by mail on forms provided by the government. They encounter government officials when they go to court, when picked up for traffic violations, when they get a driver's license, and when they mail letters at the post office. They travel on roads built by their government or in trains and air planes regulated by it. They attend state-supported schools and universities. Rubbing elbows with officialdom daily, they find their environment fixed by its functioning and its policies as much as by the weather. Reality lives in domestic politics.

In contrast to their first-hand knowledge of politics at home, the people are almost entirely without official contacts abroad. Many Americans travel as tourists in other countries, they take pictures of government buildings, and a few have occasion to deal with public officials; they may observe the domestic policies of alien governments at work but never their foreign policies. Nothing in the personal experience of Americans compares to the constant contacts of their government with other governments abroad. What they hear or read about foreign policies, whether of their own or of alien nations, can never seem as real as what they learn in the newspapers and periodicals about their own political developments at home. For these reasons the people are necessarily less hardheaded and more superficial in their thinking on foreign affairs than on domestic. And where it is difficult for them to be thoughtful, it is easy to be emotional.

Consideration of the role of the people in foreign affairs must take into account the crucial nature of foreign policy making. Mistaken domestic policies may create misery, even riots, but as a rule they can be tolerated until changed or repealed; the danger of civil war in a democracy comes less from ill-advised legislation or executive blunders than from a profound split within the populace on a subject of basic concern such as slavery. But in foreign affairs, where a government is dealing with other governments rather than with its own people, a blundering policy can be fatal. As President Kennedy once remarked, "The big difference [between domestic policies and foreign] is between a bill defeated and the country being wiped out." This fact was no doubt borne in upon his mind during the Cuban missile crisis of 1962.

The delicate nature of foreign policy making rules out, or should rule out, the political tactics which the people are in the habit of employing in domestic politics. Proponents and opponents of civil rights legislation can harangue, filibuster, parade, picket, compromise, and carry on as they will, even to the point of reflecting badly on themselves and tarnishing the nation's image abroad, without jeopardizing its very life. When such tactics are carried over into foreign affairs, be it a policy for Vietnam or elsewhere, spokesmen for the nation are frustrated and their words emptied of meaning.

The strength of the president in foreign affairs contrasts strikingly with the weakness of the people. He and his office, drawing upon the Department of State, the National Security Council, the Central Intelligence Agency, and other executive bodies, have more information bearing on policy than can be found anywhere else in the nation. He has the aid of experts, men with long experience who have the time to study alternative courses of action. He possesses an educated ear and a politician's respect for the voice of the people. And the president is committed by his oath of office to the protection of the Constitution of the United States. If by any chance he cannot be trusted to use his foreign-policy advantages wisely, the probable reason is that the people fell down on their primary democratic duty: to elect a competent, reliable man to the White House.

The contrast between the weakness of the people in foreign policy making and the strength of the president has been accentuated by the calamitous course of international relations

9

since World War I and especially since the beginning of the cold war. When committed to isolationism in world affairs, the United States had so little need for positive policies of action that the faults of our democracy in foreign affairs did not come out in the open; our procedures sufficed for the horse-and-buggy era. But after World War I shifts in the balance of power abroad forced us into the vortex of events and imposed on Washington an inescapable obligation to make vital decisions and policies. At the same time the pace of events quickened and crises precipitated by the Fascists troubled policy makers everywhere. Then after World War II the Communist-inspired cold war and the new nuclear weapons combined to infuse foreign affairs with an urgency and sensitivity hitherto unknown; American policies more than those of any other country could prevent or produce the nuclear holocaust which the world feared. Never before had skill and wisdom been so essential in the formulation of American foreign policy.

Somewhat perversely, as policy has become more demanding in skill, wisdom, and time, Americans have become more assertive, overriding their elected president and his professional assistants and dictating to them the policies the people will tolerate. The president has been captured and manacled by the new democracy while the masses have romped over his bailiwick. Members of Congress, dissatisfied as many of them have traditionally been with their part in foreign affairs and grasping for a stronger role, have aided and abetted this exercise of power by the unskilled. The Senate Foreign Relations Committee has exhibited in its open hearings a disdain for executive policies. And like the Congress, the people have fumbled wildly for more recognition and authority, uncertain of where they belong in the democratic scheme of things but sure that they are unhappy where they are. Churchmen, students, anarchists, hippies, and pacifists have filled the streets to defy the Pentagon and to destroy policies in Vietnam and the Dominican Republic. The president's powers in foreign affairs, not those of the Congress or the people, are what have been eroding.

In all candor it must be said that the president is not always right; whether he was right in Vietnam we shall not know until years hence. Nor are the president's opponents always wrong in policy issues. What must be clear, however, is that the president, with the advantages of his office, is better qualified than anybody else to be right and that he operates in foreign affairs with an assortment of motives and principles fully as sound as those within the country at large. All foreign policy, whoever its promulgator, is in some measure a gamble, and as in gambling, opinions differ on which horse will win. The question here is whose opinion will be the most reliable in the decision making that policy requires.

In the new democracy of participation there will almost certainly be dissenters from every important policy officially enunciated. If recent presidents had decided to keep out of Vietnam there would have been millions of people, at times a majority, who could be counted on to castigate them for letting the Communists overrun that country. In any vital policy effort the new democracy opens the way, therefore, to public demonstrations and coercion, whatever course of action or inaction the president takes. The issue is inescapable: can a policy serve its purpose with a perpetual attitude of hostility toward it at home, and if not, how are American interests abroad to be protected? To stifle dissension is not an acceptable way out of the problem. Rather the answer would seem to be to elevate the quality of dissension by a self-imposed discipline and by a renunciation of those methods of expression and action that invalidate government policy with no pretense of improving it or finding a credible substitute.

No mob or popular uprising can legally deprive the president of his constiutional right and duty to formulate and execute policy. But either one can make itself such a nuisance to him

11

and to the nation that in behalf of domestic tranquillity and perhaps for the sake of his own or his party's political future he feels constrained to act in violation of his judgment. Whatever success the crowd may gain in dictating the contents of a policy will, however, be the product, not of reason, democracy's ideal tool, but of its capacity to torment.

Only a strong, stubborn president can stand up against persistent popular demonstrations which appear to have the support or sympathy of a substantial percentage, majority or minority, of the people. President Washington was tested by the popular reaction to his policies during the Franco-British war, when Americans were sharply split, the Jeffersonians sympathetic to the French and the Federalists pro-British. One issue was whether the United States should go to the aid of the French. Thomas Jefferson argued that the Franco-American Alliance of 1778 obligated us to do so; Alexander Hamilton contended that the alliance was no longer binding. When the president on April 22, 1793, issued his Neutrality Proclamation, the Jeffersonians denounced it as government by proclamation and heaped abuse upon him. The president stood firm, however, and in the end his policy proved wise.

President Washington was again subjected to Jeffersonian hostility for his encounter with Citizen Genêt, sent by France as its minister to this country in 1793. Although Genêt was greeted upon his arrival in Philadelphia, the capital city, by crowds of fanatical admirers, the president, annoyed by Genêt's premature exercise of his functions in the United States, received him with cool propriety. Convinced that the president was reflecting public opinion erroneously in his stand on the French Alliance, Genêt spoke out boldly against him. Francophiles mercilessly attacked Washington, making woodcuts of him being guillotined, accusing him of wanting to be king, and concocting other such charges. In an ultramodern manner ten thousand people gathered daily in the streets of Philadelphia and threatened to drag the president out of his home, to start a revolution, or to compel the government to declare war against England. In his usual manner, the president kept his head; historian Thomas Bailey reports that Rudyard Kipling was inspired to write his poem "If" by Washington's courage at that time. Increasingly the French minister overplayed his hand, so that when the president finally demanded his recall the populace accepted it with little objection.

The Jay Treaty of 1794 was still another issue that provoked popular furor and demonstrations unfriendly to President Washington. Senators, disappointed with the draft of the treaty, decided to keep its provisions secret and to debate it in secret. They ended up by approving it, but before it could be ratified by the president, its provisions leaked out to the public. The people believed that it constituted a surrender to the English, than which nothing could be worse to post bellum patriots. At first they aimed their fury at John Jay, who was burned in effigy in many towns. Meetings of citizens adopted resolutions condemning Jay and his treaty. Trying to speak for the treaty in New York, Alexander Hamilton was stoned and forced to retreat from the platform. Popular pressure was soon directed against Washington, who was obliged to decide whether to ratify the treaty or drop it. Once again the president bravely took the harder course and concluded the treaty, knowing full well that harassment by the Jeffersonians would follow, as it did. John Randolph in a famous toast cried out, "Damn George Washington!"; and Jefferson wrote of his president in a private communication, "Curse his virtues."

Popular demonstrations during this period were largely emotional, voicing pro-French or anti-British sympathies. President Washington's policy decisions, taken over the opposition of the Francophiles, were carefully considered expressions of the national interest. The country was in no condition to take part in the war in Europe; it needed a period of peace to get on its way to becoming the great nation that it is today. The Jay Treaty, like the Neutrality Proclamation, contributed to that end; and while the treaty was in some ways unsatisfactory, it did open up new trade for Americans and a fair opportunity for financial stability and progress. The president knew what was best for the country, and he had the courage to stand up for it against the clamor of the mobs.

Other presidents have stood firm on policies which seemed to them essential to American interests. President John Adams denied those Americans who were infuriated by the XYZ affair the war with France they demanded in public meetings and by way of slogans throughout the land; like Washington, he believed that the nation needed peace to grow from infancy to healthy adulthood. Recently President Johnson, convinced that the national interest required American protection of South Vietnam against Communist aggression, stepped up the war inherited from his predecessor, over unprecedented demonstrations and protests by millions of people, usually a large minority, as the polls revealed. Recognizing that his unrelenting stand had doomed his political career, he announced in March, 1968, that he would not seek or accept the nomination of his party for reelection.

Standing up against a large, noisy, and demanding sector of the populace is an unpleasant task and one which a number of presidents have shunned. President Madison was reluctant to take the country into a war with Britain in 1812, but he was in no mood to defy the war hawks; in his message to Congress on June 1 he passed the buck to the Congress itself. The Senate voted nineteen to thirteen for war, and the House by a vote of seventy-nine to forty-nine took the same course. Thus ended the wise policy of the three preceding administrations to steer clear of war and to devote the nation's energies to the pursuits of peace.

In 1895 and 1896 President Cleveland encountered strong demands both in the country and in Congress for official recognition of Cuban belligerency and for a hostile policy toward Spain. He resisted the pressure and went so far as to say that if Congress should declare war on Spain he would not mobilize the army. When the sinking of the *Maine* in 1898 transformed the prevalent indignation into the hysteria of "Remember the *Maine*, to hell with Spain," President McKinley could not hold out against the clamor for war, although he had been committed to a peaceful solution of the Cuban problem. Reluctantly he chose the easier course and sent a war message to Congress.

It does not follow from the faults of the people that a nation must be governed by an absolute monarch, a dictator, or even an aristocracy to produce sound foreign policies. Kaiser Wilhelm II, Hitler, and Mussolini dramatized the outrageous blunders of which undemocratic governments are capable. The crimes of their regimes remind us of what can happen when the people are excluded from foreign affairs. From the opposite direction they speak, not to the need for total control by the people at the expense of their government, but rather to the need for a rational balance between the two which will utilize the contributions each can make.

Citizens are right when they stubbornly affirm that they are entitled to a place in foreign affairs, that an erroneous policy can bring them hardships—perhaps a heavier tax burden or military service and death to their youth. That the people always prefer peace while governments are inevitably bellicose is, however, an unfair assumption. In American history the people showed more enthusiasm for the War of 1812 and the Spanish-American War than did the president, and fully as much in World War I; and in the 1790s it was levelheaded presidents who kept the nation from entering the war in Europe. The argument for a popular role in policy could not be that the people will guarantee peace, but rather that they can make contributions to the quality of all policy if they can find their niche and stay in it. Within the government, between the president and Congress, there is also a balance to be achieved.

15

What is the kind of balance to be sought, first, between the people and their government, and second, between the president and the Congress within the government? Any discussion of this question must assume that the high quality in policy which has been lacking since the United States became one of the great powers following World War I is the objective in view. In government, as in an individual human being, good health is a product of sound organs functioning together in a balanced manner.

In the United States the separate organs—the president, the Congress, and the people—are strong and vital, but their total functioning is sterile; pulling in opposite directions and pushing each other about with abandon, they often appear more concerned with their self-importance than with the welfare of the nation. Working together rationally, each in its own place, they could infuse foreign policy with the decision, dispatch, and effectiveness of a dictatorship but with a firm foundation in popular sovereignty. Functioning as a unit, they could deal with the dictators in the Communist world on a better-than-even basis.

In the long run, a democracy succeeds to the degree that its people are politically sophisticated. But sophistication does not imply that the people or even the Congress should expect or try to inform themselves so well on current issues that they can take over the president's job in foreign policy. Rather it means an understanding of what they can and cannot do and the good sense to leave to the chief executive those duties for which he is best qualified and for which he is constitutionally responsible. Succinctly, the problem is to choose between two options: an undisciplined type of democracy in which the people and the Congress dominate the president to the point of vitiating or destroying his foreign-policy efforts, and a more mature democracy in which the citizens are cognizant of the special competence of their elected president and willing, without excessive meddling, to give him a chance.

3. Democratic Policy Making, 1914—45

WORLD WAR I sparked the new public interest in foreign affairs that has since fired the people to action and laid the foundations of the new democracy's policy processes. Responding to their Anglo-Saxon traditions, most Americans were sympathetic during the war to Britain and her allies, although German elements were numerous enough to make their presence felt. Official neutrality was popular as late as the election of 1916, when the slogan "He kept us out of war" appealed to voters and helped to reelect President Wilson. The subsequent resumption of un-restricted submarine warfare by Germany changed public think-ing rapidly, however, and on April 2, 1917, President Wilson went before the Congress and with great eloquence asked for a formal recognition of "the status of belligerent which has thus been thrust upon [the nation]." A new era in American foreign relations was started on its perilous way.

The increased interest of Americans in international affairs was provoked by a combination of events and circumstances. In 1917 this nation became a reluctant belligerent in a war in-stigated, so it seemed, by influences so sordid that they should be driven from the earth. In a surge of idealism Americans decided to do the job; they would make this the "War to end War," as President Wilson urged, one to make the world "safe for democracy." Stimulated by the president's advocacy of "open covenants openly arrived at" and by the prevalent tendency to blame the war on the Hohenzollern government of Germany, the people found it appealingly simple to think of war as the product of crafty diplomats and governments. The time was ripe for the people to dethrone evil and enthrone themselves.

The bickering at the Paris Peace Conference over the spoils of the war was disillusioning to many of the newly converted idealists, but it was also evidence of the need for diplomacy by the people. The thinking of some of the disenchanted turned from the League of Nations toward candidate Harding's "normalcy" and back toward the isolationism of the past. Many sought peace through disarmament or the outlawing of war. The hardier idealists continued to work for the Geneva organization even after its cause in this country was lost. But all of the newly aroused public retained their interest in world affairs, if for dissimilar reasons.

Elihu Root, who had been President Theodore Roosevelt's secretary of state, warned the people after World War I that if they were going to manage foreign affairs, they must be better informed. As though in answer to his advice, colleges and universities began in the 1920s expanding their curricula into the fields of international relations, international organization, and foreign policy. Research in these subjects quickened. Newspapers and periodicals directed attention more and more to foreign and international news. Churches, luncheon clubs, and women's organizations scheduled panel discussions and featured speeches by authorities on world affairs.

During the twenties and thirties, policy problems were plentiful; the nation could keep out of the League of Nations, but it could not detach itself from the woes of the world. Like it or not, American security, no longer ensured by a stable balance of power in Europe, had come to be tied up with problems everywhere: in Manchuria, Spain, and Ethiopia, and along the Rhine.

Reparations, war debts, currency devaluation in Britain and elsewhere, and trade barriers (including our own) pulled us irresistibly into the economics of international politics. As policy issues piled up, the alert public grew in size and influence. Democracy in foreign affairs had gained a new dimension.

Behind public debates from 1919 to 1940 over policy issues was an irreparable split between isolationists and internationalists, at first produced by the question of America's membership in the League of Nations. During the spring of 1919 the public appeared to be committed to the League, as a *Literary Digest* poll of newspaper editors indicated. Then Senator Henry Cabot Lodge and other isolationist-minded senators, although fearful that anti-League forces had no chance, went to work. Their efforts, combined with the growing disillusionment over the treaties of peace just signed in Paris, diminished the president's support in the country so much that in September, Wilson felt obliged to make a speaking tour in behalf of his cause. In the election of 1920 the people voted overwhelmingly—sixteen million to nine million—against candidate James M. Cox, the Democratic standard-bearer for the League, but with so many other issues involved, it was not clear that the election had shown a majority opinion against the League. Many analysts of the election believed that a referendum on the League issue alone in 1920 would have resulted in a victory for it, probably with some amendments.

The League was defeated in the Senate by the requirement of the Constitution that treaties be approved by a two-thirds vote. In the Senate votes during November, 1919, on an amended treaty of peace (the League Covenant included), the project did not win even a simple majority, chiefly because Democratic senators who favored it, following the president's advice, would not vote for it in its amended form. Pressure on Senator Lodge for a Senate reconsideration of the project, applied by the representatives of twenty-six prominent organizations throughout the country, led to another vote, the final one, on March 19, 1920.

At this time, with fifteen proposed amendments to the treaty, the decision was forty-nine yeas to thirty-five nays, only a few votes less than the two-thirds required. In spite of a probable majority for the treaty in the country and a demonstrated majority in the Senate, the cause was lost. This episode in which a major policy decision was dictated by a minority was upsetting to democratically minded Americans and stimulated criticism of our treaty-making process, but it was soon forgotten.

The issue of isolationism versus internationalism was again highlighted during the fight for American membership in the World Court. Presidents Wilson, Harding, Coolidge, Hoover, and Franklin Roosevelt all advocated joining the tribunal but were unable to get the requisite vote in the Senate. Although isolationists in the country were vociferous in their opposition, so much popular support for membership was expressed that both parties saw fit in the 1924 election to commit themselves to it. The House of Representatives in a resolution adopted by an impressive majority asked for membership. But in the Senate the proposal fared badly. In 1926 hard-line isolationists, as though afraid to defeat it outright, amended it fatally and then passed it with a majority well over the two-thirds required. Of the five amendments added, however, the last half of the fifth (that the Court might not, over the objection of the United States, give an advisory opinion on a question in which our government claimed an interest) was later rejected by the other members of the Court, thus leaving us out.

Swept under the carpet by the Senate in 1926, the Court issue remained there until 1935. By that time the public hauled it back into the daylight and the Senate again began hearings on membership. As deliberations progressed, strong support became apparent and at last it looked as though the United States would join. What happened at this juncture is an example of the power which the people, or a fired-up group of them, can exert over policy. Isolationist and anti-Court spokesmen, led by Father

Coughlin and the Hearst press, began a campaign of opposition to American membership. Petitions, letters, and telegrams were dispatched to senators, and speeches were made over the radio and on the platform. Pro-Court spokesmen were not organized to match this pressure. Out of it all came a Senate vote of fifty-two yeas and thirty-six nays, several short of the two-thirds needed. Once again the American version of democracy favored minority rule.

The people were much taken with the idea of disarmament during the period between the two world wars. Initiative came from the Senate, which in 1921 adopted a resolution asking for a conference of the principal naval powers. President Harding's reluctance to call a conference was overcome by the enthusiasm of the newspapers and the general public. The Washington Conference (1921–22) was followed by others at Geneva (1927 and 1932–34) and London (1930 and 1935); with diminishing optimism, the United States participated in all of these gatherings.

The net result of this preoccupation with disarmament in the 1920's and '30s was to weaken the nation's defenses at a time when crises created by Japanese aggression in the Far East and by the Nazis and the Fascists in Europe were mounting and threatening a new war. More than any other participating nation, the United States junked battleships after the Washington Conference. Then, more than any other nation, we failed to arm up to the naval limits prescribed by treaty; from 1922 to 1930 our government provided for the building of 11 warships, compared with 125 constructed by Japan and 74 by Great Britain. Even after 1934, when Congress voted to build the navy up to treaty strength, its subsequent failure to appropriate the necessary funds prolonged the weakness with which our government was obliged to meet situations of danger in the world. Realizing this, President Roosevelt asked Congress in 1938 for a billion-dollar fund to strengthen the navy. Although the Congress gave it to him, our defenses were lamentably weak when World War II broke out in 1939. The obedience of the government to the demands of the people for disarmament, however well motivated, had weakened policy in a period of crisis.

Another instance of misplaced popular enthusiasm occurred in 1927 and 1928 in behalf of the Kellogg-Briand Pact. For several years a movement had been under way in the United States for the outlawing of war. Professor James T. Shotwell, a proponent of the idea, early in 1927 suggested to French Foreign Minister Briand that war be made illegal. On April 6, the tenth anniversary of American entry into World War I, Briand proposed to the United States government a bilateral treaty in which each would agree never to go to war against the other. For months his proposal was left unanswered in the State Department, whose prolonged inaction suggested skepticism of its merits. But enthusiasts in the country for the proposal, who by this time numbered Senator William E. Borah among their leaders, began to bombard Washington with demands for action. Petitions signed by more than two million Americans were sent to government officials. The indifference of Secretary Kellogg and his advisers melted; he not only replied favorably to Briand's proposal but suggested that the renunciation of war be placed on a multilateral rather than a bilateral basis. This was done, and on August 27, 1928, the pact renouncing war as an instrument of policy was signed by the representatives of fifteen nations; many other nations later adhered to it.

The people of the United States rejoiced, knowledgeable people who believed that by a stroke of the pen war had at last been laid to rest, an eternal rest. Only a few Americans pointed out the pact's defects—its lack of machinery to prevent war, its silence on the complex causes of war, and its admission that nations might fight in self-defense. The critics noted that all nations at war are prone to think of their objective as self-defense. After casting his vote for it in the Senate, Senator Carter Glass expressed a hope that his fellow Americans would not think him so naive as to consider the pact "worth a postage stamp." With the passing of time, the wars, declared and undeclared, in China, Ethiopia, and Europe revealed the accuracy of the senator's assessment. Instead of abolishing wars, the pact at best discouraged declarations and encouraged the claim of self-defense for what appeared to be aggression. The experience could hardly inspire admiration for democracy's skill in foreign affairs.

In the 1930s, as Japan, Italy, and Germany maneuvered humanity ever closer toward a new world war, the American people, in a peace-at-any-price mood, determined to insulate themselves against involvement. This "national neutrality neurosis," as it has been called, was founded partially on a conviction that our part in World War I had been a horrible mistake which must not be repeated. Behind it, too, were the findings of the Nye Committee (1934–35) in the Senate, the gist of which was that the munitions makers, the "merchants of death," had used their influence in government to get us into World War I with the purpose of making profits.

In 1935 the Congress, in answer to the demands of Americans, enacted the first of a series of neutrality laws designed to keep us out of the next war by giving up the neutral rights for which President Wilson had stood firm from 1914 to 1917; it would prevent the sale or transportation to a belligerent of munitions, the extension of loans to a belligerent, and travel by Americans on belligerent ships. President Roosevelt had asked the Congress for authority to deny munitions to aggressors while allowing their purchase by the victims of aggression, but public opinion demanded identical treatment to both sides. The president reluctantly signed the bill.

When war broke out in 1939, the Neutrality Act, revised in 1936 and 1937, did not seem to most people as commendable as it had earlier. Many Americans sympathized with Britain and France, as did President Roosevelt, convinced that only an Allied

23

victory could ensure the future of civilization; but the law prevented this country from translating sympathy into tangible aid. The American public discovered that what it had thought in 1935–37 it wanted for the future was not what it actually wanted when that future arrived. The nations whose cause now seemed just were prevented by the existing embargo on the sale of munitions to all belligerents from buying even so much as a single gun, either from American manufacturers or from our government. To change all this, President Roosevelt called the Congress into special session in 1939 and recommended the repeal of the arms embargo, together with the reenactment of two provisions of the Neutrality Act (the "cash and carry" requirement for belligerents in the purchase of goods, and the prohibition of American ships and persons from going into danger zones) which had lapsed.

Reacting to these proposals, the country and the Congress began one of the "great debates" of our diplomatic history. Feeling ran high as interventionists and noninterventionists tangled in a war of words and tempers. The former were convinced that, although the interests of the United States were on the side of the democracies, we were in fact helping the dictators (who had stored up vast supplies of the hardware of war before starting hostilities) by withholding supplies from the needy democracies that had gone into the conflict relatively unprepared. The latter maintained that it would be blatantly unneutral to change the rules after the fighting had started, for the purpose of helping one side against the other. The former opposed legislation designed to keep American ships and passengers out of danger zones, whereas the latter regarded it as essential if we were to avoid being dragged into the conflict. The compromise act of November, 1939, repealed the embargo and reenacted the danger-zone provision.

The neutrality legislation of 1935–39 was one of democracy's least successful ventures in foreign affairs. To the extent that it was based upon the widespread belief that the manufacture and sale of munitions was the principal cause for our entry into World War I, it was a gross oversimplification both of the events of 1914–17 and of the causes of war in general; it reflected a proclivity toward the superficial in world affairs. The legislation was a renunciation of responsibility for the future course of events; no matter who annihilated whom, it would be none of our business. It assumed a capacity for a detachment from world events which no people could attain, and an inactivity in the midst of a spreading upheaval which no great nation could impose upon itself. It told the world that any nation might upset the balance of power anywhere, even to our detriment, without our batting an eye. To be more concrete, it notified Hitler and Mussolini that, conquer as they pleased, we would stand idly by, not even allowing Britain and France, the probable victims, to buy goods from us in accordance with long-established practices of international law.

To say that the neutrality statutes of 1935–39 sparked World War II would be far-fetched, but no one could doubt that the dictators were comforted to have an assurance that we would stay out of it. Had we been consistent and stayed out, a policy of neutrality would have made some sense. But as it turned out, we gave the dictators every reason to believe that we would take an aloof position in the next war which in fact we did not take. Democracy's policy proved misleading at a time when clarity and precision would have made a contribution to peace.

From 1939 until Pearl Harbor, American policy was characterized by the same uncertainty and confusion. Both in the country and in Washington we wavered, not clear about the direction in which we should move or even whether we should move at all. The United States was a giant paralyzed by indecision, with enough sense to worry but not enough to think confidently and fearlessly toward a tenable position. The debaters were the interventionists, or internationalists, and the noninterventionists, or isolationists. The issue was to what extent, if at all, this country should aid the cause of the British and French in their defense against the dictators. Opinions ranged all the way from the belief that we should join the Allied cause in war to the opposite extreme, which advocated giving no help that would constitute a violation either of the traditional international law on neutrality or of the American neutrality law. Most Americans, however, were for limited aid, approving Roosevelt's description of the United States as the "arsenal of democracy." Shortly before the president made the "destroyer-bases" deal in 1940 with Britain (to give her fifty overage destroyers in return for military bases in the British Caribbean islands), a Gallup poll found that 62 percent of the people favored the existing policy while 38 percent opposed it. The effect on public thinking of the fall of France in June, 1940, had, by the time the poll was taken, added to the strength of the interventionists.

Gradually the Arsenal of Democracy became more and more committed to the defense of the embattled Allies through acts that were unneutral by any standard. The assets in the United States of Denmark, Norway, and other countries overrun by the Nazis were frozen, their governments-in-exile were recognized, British pilots were permitted to train in Florida, and Allied warships were allowed to make repairs in our ports. In January, 1941, the Lend-Lease Act was passed, by which aid to the Allies was both expanded and systematized. All this was done in the midst of a nation-wide debate. The pro-aid group argued that the Allies could and would do the job of defeating the enemy with our material aid and that in this way we could stay out of the fighting. The America First people were sure that the escalation of our aid would inevitably bring us into battle. To prevent passage of the Lend-Lease bill, mothers marched up the steps of the Capitol building carrying signs petitioning Congress to kill the bill, not their boys. Senator Burton K. Wheeler, a leader of the isolationists, denounced the bill as a plan "to plow under every fourth American boy."

The Lend-Lease program inevitably edged this nation closer to war; to lend and lease goods to the Allies would be futile unless deliveries could be made. In April, 1941, the president established naval patrols which informed British warships and planes of the location of German submarines. Our navy convoyed goods to Iceland, where British warships undertook to protect them on the rest of the route. Roosevelt announced a little later that we would shoot at sight German submarines found within a "defensive zone" which he had defined. The majority of the public went along with such measures—a Gallup poll in June, 1941, found a decisive majority in favor of the convoy—but a large and boisterous minority opposed them.

The issue of what the attitude of the United States should be to the war in Europe was not debated in the dispassionate and reasoned manner that would be associated with democracy at its best. The argument was emotional and bitter; there were, for instance, pastors of churches who were ousted because they differed with leading members of their congregations on the issue of intervention. Our actual policy was what a president who believed that the security of this nation was inextricably tied up with the changing balance of power in Europe could devise without converting a minority of opponents into a devastating majority; it was not what the president, with his fingers on the pulse of world events, wanted, but rather what he could get by with in the country.

Not the president or the people, but the Japanese at Pearl Harbor on December 7, 1941, made the final decision on the role of the United States in World War II. And although proof on the point is not available, it is possible that the Japanese decided as they did because they saw in the American people an indecision and confusion which to them reflected weakness. Our considerable ability to acquire a purpose and a determination when attacked by an external enemy is a national quality difficult for others to understand. To the dictators in 1941, American

27

weakness was not only one of will but also one of actual military capability, for we had failed to prepare adequately for war during our flirtation with disarmament and neutrality legislation.

War came to the United States in 1941, first, because aggressive dictators were on the loose, and second, because democracy's foreign policies were weak, without foresight, purpose, and decision. The people's reliance on the Pact of Paris, neutrality, and disarmament blinded them to the machinations of Hitler and Mussolini, who trusted in a quick victory before the United States could arm. Japan felt able to dismiss America as a serious opponent in the Far East, once our fleet had been annihilated at Pearl Harbor. That the government in Washington, especially President Roosevelt, had made a more accurate assessment of current events than either the people or the Congress and sought a more realistic policy is apparent from his effort to get the Congress to build up the armed forces and from his attempt to have the Congress incorporate into the neutrality legislation of 1935 a provision enabling him to discriminate in wartime against the trade of aggressors.

4. Democratic Policy Making, 1945—70

During World War II the people's main interest in world affairs was to defeat the enemy. The emergency of war found the generals, the policy makers, and the people pulling together effectively for the common cause. Idealism about the new world to come was moderate in comparison with the wild optimism of 1917–19, but government projects for a new international organization elicited interest, especially in religious and intellectual quarters. Private societies and groups constructed draft charters, as did the State Department, and they deliberated on aspects of possible terms of the peace settlement presumed to be ahead— boundary lines, reparations, trade arrangements, the status of colonial areas, and war crimes. In the election of 1944, nothing seemed to matter so much as whether it was "time for a change"; in foreign affairs, debate centered on the issue of whether the Democrats or the Republicans were the better qualified to bring the war to an end and make peace. Wartime democracy was equal to its task in world affairs.

Since World War II, American policy makers have been busy coping with the aggressive moves of the Communists. In this cold war they have faced a never ending series of crises and an untold number of lesser issues such as cultural exchanges, payment of United Nations expenses, repayment by Russia of her lend-lease obligations to us, and the admission of Communist China to the

United Nations. Since 1945, both the people and the Congress have shown great concern over the direction which American policies have taken and have challenged the president on many of his decisions. As never before, democracy's capability in foreign policy making has been tested.

A public opinion of some kind has been expressed on every issue of significance. Sometimes the "public" has been a small one; not many Americans concerned themselves with the issue of the United Nations debts for peace-keeping, nor were there any parades or teach-ins on the subject. A larger public intruded itself in the questions of recognizing Communist China and admitting her to the United Nations. Crises which involved or threatened to involve the nation in hostilities—Korea, Berlin, Cuba, the Dominican Republic, the Congo, and Vietnam—were the issues which excited Americans, and it is in such crises that the president often had to act quickly, taking his chances on what the reaction of the people or the Congress would be. For instance, when the Communists invaded South Korea on June 25, 1950, President Truman quickly ordered our naval and air forces to give aid to the beleaguered country, even before the Security Council of the United Nations could be called together; had he waited for discussions by the Security Council, the Congress, or the people, it would have been too late. Most of the Congress and the American people gave strong backing to the president's action, but the polls showed that a sizable minority followed Senator Robert Taft in opposition to the "war."

Presidents Truman, Eisenhower, and Kennedy enjoyed substantial support for their stands on the Berlin issue, although many Americans thought that Kennedy might have taken measures to prevent the Communists from building the wall in the city. President Kennedy's demand that Russia get her missiles out of Cuba met with little opposition in the country, but his failure to act sooner and his unwillingness at the time of the crisis to demand that the Communists (including Castro) get out of Cuba forthwith encountered lively indignation from elements of the public. President Johnson's decisive action in landing marines in the Dominican Republic to prevent, as he believed, a Communist takeover was condemned by many Americans convinced that American intervention was immoral and illegal and fearful that the government was veering into a course of irresponsible use of its great power. The Vietnamese ventures of the United States stimulated what have probably been the most violent assertions of public concern in our history.

The government in Washington showed a keen interest in developments in Vietnam even while the French were still there, concerned lest the end of French rule open the way to Communist control; for this reason it donated three billion dollars worth of arms to the French cause. A Gallup poll at that time found that 56 percent of the people were agreeable to this move while 28 percent opposed it. After the French defeat at Dienbienphu, our government took part in a conference of nineteen nations at Geneva in 1954 to discuss the future of Indochina. The partition of Vietnam along the 17th parallel by the conference did not bring the stability expected, and it was not long before the Communists of North Vietnam were organizing the Viet Cong and directing its attacks in South Vietnam. The response of the United States government to this aggression was to give military advice and assistance against the Viet Cong to the government in Saigon. From that point on, the process of escalation began on both sides until troops from the Communist North, supported by Peking and Moscow, became directly involved on an increasing scale and the armed forces of the United States were deployed to the area in growing numbers.

The reaction of the public was calm and contained until American soldiers were sent to Vietnam, when debate began and grew apace until it occupied almost the whole arena of politics. Both the hawks, who contended that we had no acceptable alternative to fighting, and the doves, who opposed escalation or even advocated withdrawal from Vietnam, have given full vent to their convictions. Actually, public opinion has been more fragmented than split, for there have been several breeds of hawks and several of doves. In this free-for-all, democracy's handicaps in foreign affairs came out in full view. They again press upon us the question of whether the people can guide to success the nation's foreign policy in a world disrupted by the ambitions of powerful Communist states.

The public opinion polls taken after the president began sending troops to Vietnam have revealed a substantial and usually a majority support for his policy, as well as a strong opposition, the exact size of both changing from time to time. In late April, 1966, according to a Harris poll, 62 percent of the people supported administration policy, 29 percent opposed it, and 9 percent were unsure of themselves. The April poll also showed 43 percent favoring escalation of hostilities as against 48 percent opposing it, almost exactly reversing the figures taken two months earlier. Obviously, the president was under fire both from the "get-out-now" crowd and from the "get-it-over-quick" escalators. A Gallup poll published on September 25, 1966, reported that 18 percent of the people favored withdrawing American troops, 18 percent wished to carry on hostilities at the existing level, 55 percent advocated stronger pressure on the Communists, and 9 percent had no opinion. At this point the escalators clearly were gaining. But as the war dragged on without a decision, casualties mounted and criticism abroad became more furious. Support for the president began to diminish.

Dr. Gallup reported that in September, 1967, only 38 percent approved the way the president was handling his job (including the war in Vietnam) and 50 percent disapproved. Two months later these figures had changed, with 46 percent approving and 41 percent disapproving. From this point on, percentages continued to disclose a public sharply divided not only on the war itself but also on questions of strategy and tactics. A Gallup poll published on October 16, 1969, the day after the peace moratorium, showed that 57 percent of the people questioned were satisfied with President Nixon's performance in the White House, 24 percent were dissatisfied, and 19 percent had no opinion.

Differences of opinion within a democracy—or for that matter, within a dictatorship—are not surprising or reprehensible. It was the manner in which those differences were expressed—the lack of restraint, the ill will, dogmatism, emotionalism, noise, and display, rarely infused with impressive reasoning—that stunned democracy's admirers. Quite naturally these excesses were committed more by opponents of presidential policy, bent upon forcing a change, than by supporters who were more or less satisfied with it.

Among the weapons used in this struggle for the control of American policy were the old, familiar ones: letters, telegrams, debates, editorials, petitions, and resolutions to gain the attention of the public or of officialdom in Washington. Peace organizations, church leaders, student groups, educators, and others who thought they had found a simple solution to a complicated problem bombarded the government with pronouncements and resolutions. Accusations were leveled at the government that it was withholding facts from the public, that it was evading honest requests from the Communists to negotiate, and that it was trying to police the world. Nationally known senators, congressmen, editors, professors, and columnists engaged in nation-wide controversy. Individuals and groups bought space in the newspapers, often a full page, to advertise their views on what the government ought to do or on what it was doing that was wrong. Pickets marched in front of the White House and parades filled the streets of our cities. Peace-minded enthusiasts obstructed military traffic and blocked entrances to buildings.

This "great debate" also called forth new weapons of attack and defense. In the summer of 1965 a number of congressmen scheduled unofficial hearings in their respective districts at which proponents and opponents of American policy were free to express their views; some of them, like the one held at Queens Borough Hall in New York, were heavily charged with anger directed against either the government or its critics. College and university students, traditionally aloof from the "great debates" of the nation, scheduled teach-ins, usually loaded in advance with antigovernment ammunition. The week end of October 15–16, 1965, for instance, was devoted to demonstrations, teach-ins, and parades on scores of campuses and in many cities as well. To counterbalance the effect of these activities, the proponents of American policy held in Washington on October 16 what its sponsors called the first national teach-in supporting United States policy in Vietnam; an estimated five hundred students from forty college and university campuses in twenty states listened to speeches by Senator Thomas Dodd, Ambassador Tran Van Chuong, and others. These demonstrations continued throughout 1966, 1967, 1968, and 1969 (directed in 1969 against the president's peace-making policies). One of the most serious was that held in Chicago during the Democratic Convention of 1968, which rocked the nation from end to end.

The most novel of all the demonstrations of protest was the peace moratorium organized by a committee in which a few supporters of Senator Eugene V. McCarthy's presidential campaign were prominent. It was planned as a nation-wide effort on a grass-roots basis to force the president to speed up his program of disengagement from Vietnam. The demonstrations scheduled for October 15, 1969, were to be followed one month later by two days of protest, two months later by three days, and so on, adding one day in every succeeding month. The demonstrations of October 15 included parades, speeches, informal discussions, and public readings of lists of war dead; several million people took part in the day's activities. In the historic Boston Common alone one hundred thousand Americans assembled to display their displeasure with President Nixon's policy.

Prominent among the critics of the government were church leaders and educators. In sermons and in resolutions by church groups, including the National Council of Churches, clergymen challenged what they believed to be an immoral policy of bloodshed and devastation in Vietnam. On May 12, 1965, several hundred Protestant, Catholic, and Jewish leaders gathered together and marched across the Potomac to the Pentagon, where they appealed to Secretary McNamara to stop the bombing of North Vietnam and begin negotiations to end the war. A group of Americans which included many church leaders signed an advertisement placed in a number of newspapers condemning the bombing; it was headed by the caption "Mr. President—In the Name of God, Stop it!" The *Christian Century* in its editorials and in its published articles by clergymen denounced both the war itself as unethical and the manner in which the American government was fighting it—the escalation, the use of napalm, and the bombing. At the Uppsala Assembly of the World Council of Churches in July, 1968, the American delegation, headed by Dr. Robert Brown, engineered the adoption of a resolution condemning American policy and demanding that "the mortal suffering of the Vietnamese people should at once be ended." These Americans rejected proposals that the other side also be denounced.

On June 5, 1966, a group of 6,400 educators and other leaders published in the *New York Times* what was believed to be the largest political advertisement ever run in a newspaper, calling on the government to stop offensive military operations immediately and "to evaluate seriously" a plan of self-determination for the Vietnamese people. The signatures to the three-page appeal included those of 3,936 faculty members from 180 colleges and universities; this academic roster counted 190 names from Columbia University, 176 from Harvard, and 165 from New York University, many of scholars of distinction. Prominent educators and faculty groups in 1969 were still loudly vocal in their opposition to the war and to the manner in which it was conducted.

In Congress the debate over Vietnam was quite as impassioned as in the country, although the president was given the legislation and money needed for his policy. Opposition to President Johnson's policy was voiced by members of both parties, but more came from his own Democratic party than from the Republicans; some Republicans advocated an even tougher line in Vietnam. His severest opposition came from members of the Senate Foreign Relations Committee, and especially the chairman, Senator J. William Fulbright. To educate the people, as he believed, his committee held televised hearings on Vietnam and other issues of policy, presenting spokesmen both of the government and of the opposition, but harrying the former more than the latter. On the floor of the Senate and in the country, he and his supporters lashed out against government policy.

Senator Fulbright believed that he was not being "irresponsible," but rather that it was his duty, however unpleasant, to offer to the president, "the best advice" he could on policy, and that this duty took "precedence over party loyalty"; the absence of substantial criticism from the Republicans, the opposition party, rendered it imperative, so he argued, that criticism emanate from other quarters. Incongruous as it might seem, it was not the first time that a chairman of the powerful Senate Foreign Relations Committee deserted his president and party leaders; during the Civil War, Senator Charles Sumner embarrassed Secretary of State Seward and the Lincoln administration, who were trying to play down the issue of the French in Mexico, by a wild speech against Emperor Napoleon III; and in April, 1869, he had a large part in the defeat of the Johnson-Clarendon Treaty negotiated by Seward to settle the *Alabama* claims controversy and supported by the new Grant administration. Senator Fulbright criticized President Johnson's policies not only in Vietnam but also in the Dominican Republic, Thailand, Communist China, and on foreign aid.

The excesses of those critics who have made up the opposition to the government from 1965 to 1970 may be ascribed to a misunderstanding of the cold war as well as to the people's ignorance of their legitimate place in the formulation of democracy's foreign policy. The term "cold war" is disarming; it sounds interestingly odd but like something not to be taken too seriously. It disguises the fact that the Communists want to destroy democracy and absorb the free world. We have been in the cold war so long—for more than the entire lifetime of most college students—that we readily discount its fatal potentialities, especially when the Soviet Union is in a smiling mood.

As a democracy, we fight the cold war under an inherent disadvantage: whereas the Soviet Union and Red China are not obliged to keep their people's fighting spirit up because their cold-war battles are fought by governments not accountable to the public, in a democracy the people must be kept alert and tense to support the war effort. But in fact no way can be found to keep two hundred million Americans in a fighting mood for more than twenty years plus an indefinite period in the future; and we would all be emotional wrecks if a way were found. Bringing a peacetime psychology to cold-war problems, Americans wrangle with each other and with their government, which, closer to world events and at the same time charged with the responsibility for the security of the nation, feels a need for vigorous action.

Anxious that their peace be more perfect, some Americans from 1965 to 1970 have tried to convince themselves and others that the cold war is over, that the Soviet Union has become a responsible member of the international community and no longer should be feared. At the time when these people were telling Washington to stop worrying about the Communists, our government was fighting an enemy in Vietnam supplied with Soviet weapons, struggling in the United Nations to induce Russia to support the peace-keeping operations of the organization, encountering Soviet efforts to penetrate the Middle East, and keeping a watchful eye on Communist raids across the 38th parallel in Korea. The Russian invasion of Czechoslovakia in 1968 and renewed pressure on Berlin in 1969 raised doubts in the minds of some Americans about the termination of the cold war, but attitudes toward government policies were little affected.

Disdainful of the cold war, dissenters have grown impatient with their government for continuing to fight it. But to those who believe they see the cold war going on all about them—and this includes most of the policy makers in Washington—dissenters appear to blame those who oppose aggression more for world disorder than those who commit it. Distrustful of their government for its inability to establish normalcy, they attempt to usurp its functions. This they did on Vietnam policy.

Never has the foreign-policy process seemed so out of balance as in the period from 1965 through 1969. The president's policy of limited hostilities in Vietnam, no doubt adopted out of fear of the criticism at home and abroad that more decisive military action might provoke, called for more patience and endurance than the people could muster. In the unrest and disorder which developed, the policy enunciated by the president could not seem credible to the enemy or to the world at large, nor could he find another that would do even a minimal part of what he believed needed to be done. Democracy was paralyzed, unable to speak for itself.

5. The People's Approach to Policy

As THE FOREGOING chapters have shown, since World War I the people have been striving for and gaining control over American foreign policy. Indignant at what seems to them excessive presidential power, unwisely exercised, they have been subverting the constitutional arrangement of authority which recognizes the inherent advantages of the chief executive in foreign affairs. The strategy, as noted earlier, is for the people so to hedge the president about with political obstructions that he cannot use his authority freely.

Popular interest in foreign affairs, we may safely assume, has been patriotic and honorable, with only a sprinkling of individuals driven by baser motives. German sympathizers in the two world wars were not numerous, nor did they count much in public thinking. Americans who have opposed their government's policies during the cold war are, for the most part, loyal citizens who have not sold out to the Communists, although they have advocated policies which have appeared beneficial to the enemy's cause; to be sure, among their number are a few hard-core Communists and fellow travelers.

The fault of the people in foreign affairs has not been a lack of good faith but their shortcomings in temperament and skill. In their performance to date, serious limitations in their capacity to deal with foreign policy issues have stood out, limitations which point to a more modest role in the policy-making process than that which they covet. To expect the people to overcome their limitations and perfect their capability would be both to overestimate human nature and to underestimate the complexities of decision making in foreign affairs. It would be rather like asking the whole populace to become nuclear physicists or proficient golfers.

From President Washington's time to Richard Nixon's, the usual response of the people to foreign policy issues has been either indifference or emotionalism. Isolationism and indifference were the two sides of the same coin. The lesser issues that are not played up on the front pages of the papers—and these include potential major problems, such as Vietnam—from 1954 to 1964—never have had and probably never will have much attention. Issues that have already become important stimulate an excited response within the nation.

President Washington met with passionate pro-French and pro-British attitudes in his efforts to be pro-American in his policies toward Europe. In his Farewell Address (1796), he devoted four full paragraphs to the pitfalls in foreign affairs of "an habitual hatred or an habitual fondness" for another nation. He believed that "a nation prompted by ill will and resentment sometimes impels to war the government contrary to the best calculations of policy." Sympathy for another nation, he argued, causes "the illusion of an imaginary common interest in cases where no real common interest exists, and infusing into one the enmities of the other, betrays the former into a participation in the quarrels and wars of the latter without adequate inducement or justification."

President Adams, in his desire to prevent war, struggled with an emotional public angry at France over the XYZ affair. Later the war hawks, infuriated by a series of hostile acts by the British on the high seas, were too much for President Madison to handle, and therefore he let Congress choose between war and peace.

So has it been on down to the present, as with an overheated fervor we have been fighting each other over American policy in Vietnam.

In *The Man in the Street* (1948), Thomas Bailey, discussing American attitudes toward foreign affairs, had much to say about the "bumptiousness" of the early Americans, sectionalism, Anglophobia, suspicion of foreigners, and other emotionalized attitudes behind American behavior. Noting that "the war of 1914–18 was a delectable dish for the professional emotionalist," he recalled some of the emotionalized words and phrases of the period: "atrocities," "holy war," "Huns," and "Hang the Kaiser." The sacred cows of our history such as manifest destiny, isolationism, and the Monroe Doctrine have always fed more on the people's emotions—pride, daring, and conceit—than upon a rational understanding of the national interest.

As former Secretary of State Acheson has recently said, many Americans are so volatile that they readily succumb to hysteria. In World War I superpatriots banned German music and removed the German language from the curricula of schools and colleges. We like to find scapegoats against whom we can rail: munitions makers, the president, or the Pentagon. Today's protesters against presidential policy in Vietnam frequently display great emotion, even to the point of hysteria!

Emotional sprees are not peculiar to Americans. The stable Englishman was quite as rabid in his hatred of the Germans in 1914–18 as we, and it was this fact that compelled David Lloyd George to make exorbitant demands for reparations and other punitive measures at the Paris Peace Conference. Those Frenchmen who supported de Gaulle were, like him, imbued with a national pride which led them to resent American influence in Europe and to strive for a position of leadership on the continent. The people of the Democratic Republic of China appear to have gone mad in their hatred of the West, especially of the United States.

41

One curse of emotionalism in the body politic is that it minimizes reason. Not only are a wrought-up people themselves incapable of reasoning, but, what is worse, they make it difficult for their government to reason and to adjust policies to the national interest, which should at all times be its guide. As Professor Charles Lerche has said, "Emotions bulk large in American international attitudes," and for that reason "it is difficult to maintain mass enthusiasm for the controlling constant of national interest; the public most likely follows the course dictated by current likes and dislikes."

If emotions have a legitimate role in foreign affairs, it is not to fix the substance of policy. They can be a stimulant to action but never a determinant of the kind of action to be taken. Anger and fear when it was found that Russia had installed missiles in Cuba could demand that something be done about them, but only reason could devise a prudent policy. For a nation to act blindly when emotionally upset, as a small boy will likely do, can be disastrous to its welfare. For the United States to decide petulantly to cut off foreign aid to nations that fail to display gratitude or to support our policies would be to ignore the reasonable purposes of the program, such as strengthening weaker nations so that they will be immune to Communism and bolstering the satellite countries in their effort to throw off Russian domination.

Observers of American foreign policy also often condemn the absorption with ethical principles and the deprecation of the national interest and power which they have found to be prevalent within the body politic. In his *American Diplomacy, 1900–1950,* Ambassador George Kennan regretted "the legalistic-moralistic approach to international problems" which he alleged "runs like a red skein through our foreign policy of the last fifty years." Professor Hans Morgenthau listed four erroneous intellectual attitudes which he believes have affected American thinking

on foreign policy since World War II: utopianism, legalism, senti-
mentalism, and neoisolationism. Professor Dexter Perkins in *The
American Approach to Foreign Policy* also revealed in some detail this penchant of Americans for moralizing.

Indifference even more than morality characterized the attitude of Americans toward foreign affairs during the period of
isolationism before World War I. Ethics were not lacking in
what public concern there was for policies, but there was not
much concern. There were not enough howls of indignation in
1848 to prevent President Polk from taking a large piece of land
from Mexico, but there was enough morality in the country and
in Congress to convince him that it would be best to pay for the
acquisition. When Theodore Roosevelt employed questionable
methods to get the right to build the Panama Canal in 1903,
there was no public uproar, but there was enough newspaper
criticism of his tactics so that he felt obliged to rationalize his
conduct by blaming the Bogota government for its weakness and
by insisting that the canal would prove to be a boon to all mankind. As isolationism and indifference have given way to popular
involvement in foreign affairs, the door has been opened wider
and wider to the moralism of today.

Almost as though it were a matter of instinct, public thinking
on foreign policy turns into ethical channels. When Americans
came into world affairs so enthusiastically during World War I,
their purpose, it will be remembered, was to purify international
relations. This tendency of all peoples to espouse the "good" and
to abhor "evil" explains why it is that governments label their
policies with impressive phrases: the "open door policy," "freedom of the seas," the "good neighbor policy," the "new order in
Europe," and "war of liberation." Such labels are intended by
governments to gain the backing of the people just as are charges,
true or false, that the enemy is committing "aggression" or is
guilty of "atrocities." Rarely does a government dare to come out
and admit unethical or illegal conduct, as Chancellor von Beth-

mann-Hollweg did on August 4, 1914, when he said about the German invasion of Belgium, "The wrong—I speak openly—that we are committing we will make good as soon as our military goal has been reached"; the chancellor no doubt hoped that his promise to "make good" Germany's delinquency would satisfy the people both at home and abroad.

No one can denounce the people for striving to be ethical and for holding up a high standard of conduct for governments. But in the world as it is, with popular control of policy weak in the Communist dictatorships and strong in the democracies, the terms of competition become quite uneven. The Communists play the game by one set of rules and we by another, and the stakes are high. What is the answer? Should democracies hold themselves to a high standard of conduct with a grave risk to the security of the free world, while their enemies, unhampered by an ethically minded public, engage in any practice that will promote their ambitions? Can America eschew force as unethical while Communists employ it? Although the answers of conscientious people to these questions differ, few would push moralism so far as to jeopardize the life of the nation. The question is how much of a risk is tolerable. It is understandable that a moralistic public is willing to take a greater risk than is their government, on whom the responsibility for the protection of the nation has been placed. Only time will tell whether today's moralists are too obstructive to government policies of self-defense.

What is most to be deplored in discussions of American foreign policy is not a sensitivity to moral principles but an indifference to any or all of the other considerations that enter into prudent decision making. Policy is not merely a matter of right and wrong; it is also a matter of security and self-protection, of economic welfare, of capability (being able to do what is attempted), of foretelling the reactions of others, of intelligence (obtaining and utilizing information), of harmonizing what is to be attempted in one part of the world with what is being done in other parts, and of adjusting action abroad so as to minimize conflict with desirable domestic programs. To be absorbed solely with the ethical aspect of policy runs the risk not only of unwise policies but also of steeling the popular mind against the compromises essential to international relations, for moral principles, once determined to be applicable in a given situation, are unbending. Furthermore, the question of what is ethical in a concrete policy problem is as debatable in the relations of nations as in the conduct of individuals. Is it, for instance, more ethical to desist from the use of force in Vietnam than to use it and prevent the Communists from inching their way throughout Southeast Asia? In the Middle East would the United States conform more closely to ethical standards by selling arms to Israel alone, to the Arab states alone, to both the Arab states and Israel, or to neither?

For a government like ours to devise a workable foreign policy in the midst of a people whose only thought is morality poses a stubborn problem. As Assistant Secretary of State Harlan Cleveland said in 1962 in an address to the Federation of Woman's Clubs, "Sometimes the introduction of pure ideals rather interferes with the clarity of vision." Former Secretary of State Acheson recently wrote, from a wealth of experience in policy making, "The righteous who seek to deduce foreign policy from ethical or moral principles are as misleading and misled as the modern Machiavellis who would conduct our foreign relations without regard to them." As he sees it, the overriding guide to policy should be "the strategic approach—to consider various courses of action from the point of view of their bearing upon major policy objectives." This, as he noted, was President Lincoln's political philosophy. Much as Lincoln hated slavery as unethical, his first objective was to save the Union; in a letter to Horace Greeley he wrote, "If I could save the Union without freeing any slave, I would do it; and if I could save it by freeing some and leaving others alone, I would also do that." Another expert in statecraft,

Prime Minister Winston Churchill, when queried about the morality of fighting as an ally of Communist Russia during World War II, answered that he would make an ally of the devil if by so doing he could hasten a victory over the Nazis; he kept a steady eye on his major objective.

The preoccupation with ethical principles characteristic of the American people is evident in nearly all popular discussions of foreign policy. Listen to two Americans arguing about President Johnson's dispatch of marines to the Dominican Republic and you hear them talking about whether or not it was an indecent act of domination by a powerful nation over a weak neighbor, "intervention" in violation of treaty commitments, the kind of action that Russia took in Hungary in 1956, or a case of might making right. Debate over policy in Vietnam has revolved about the horror of war, the wickedness of the bombing, "policing the world," "intervention" in what is said to be a civil war, "aggression," the failure to hold an election as prescribed by the Geneva Agreement of 1954, and reluctance to negotiate. And these discussions of ethics have centered on American policy, unconcerned about the ruthless tactics of North Vietnam or the National Liberation Front.

What has been neglected, if not ignored, in popular discussions of the Vietnam issue is the interests of the United States and the free world. Little if any thought has been directed to such considerations as (1) evidence of Communist intentions in Thailand, Cambodia, Malaysia, and other parts of Southeast Asia; (2) evidences that India might or might not be able to withstand a Communist surge in neighboring Southeast Asia; (3) the effect on American defense of the Philippines (to which we are committed) if the Asiatic mainland nearby were to fall to the Communists; (4) the effect on the military balance and on trade in the Far East if strategic Singapore were in hostile hands; and (5) whether the United States is capable of defending South Vietnam while at the same time meeting its NATO commitments and maintaining its domestic programs.

Presidents, responsible more than anybody else for the security of America, cannot slough off questions relating to the national interest without opening themselves to criticism for their negligence. In devising and maintaining their policy of protection of South Vietnam, Presidents Kennedy, Johnson, and Nixon might well have remembered that the Truman-Acheson government was criticized for not doing more to protect mainland China from Communism in 1945–49, and that Republicans in Congress demanded an investigation into what many believed had been a neglect of the national interest. The chief executive is the one person who cannot afford to get bogged down in a fruitless debate with himself on what is "good" and what is "bad," to the neglect of the national interest. Were he to do so he could open himself to impeachment for his failure to defend the nation.

Justifying their preoccupation with the ethics of policy, many Americans would argue that the national interest is a sordid basis for policy, especially for a people who profess to be Christian. President Wilson said to an audience at Mobile in 1913, "It is a perilous thing to determine the foreign policy of a nation in the terms of material interest. It is not only unfair to those with whom you are dealing, but it is degrading as regards your own action." He went on to say, "We have no selfish ends to serve. . . . We are but one of the champions of the rights of mankind." What he meant by "material interest" is not clear. Certainly neither he nor anybody else would advocate self-abnegation in foreign policy. Indeed his own policy was anything but self-abnegating, for he and Secretary of State Bryan committed themselves vigorously to the protection of American interests, financial and otherwise, in Latin America. The president worked for nearly three years to safeguard the trade of Americans, a profitable trade, with belligerent nations; and when he went before

47

Congress on April 2, 1917, to ask for a declaration of war against Germany, he was motivated, according to many historians, not only by high aspirations for an end to all war, but also by a fear for the future of American security in a world dominated by Germany. Despite his idealism, he did not abjure in his policies what he believed to be the interests of his country.

Beyond doubt, a nation may so construe the national interest as to make it both sordid and aggressive. Hitler's conception of the German national interest called for the annihilation of the free nations of Europe and unrestrained expansion. Japan at the same time saw her national interest as demanding domination of the Far East. The Communist world revolution is equally oblivious of the sovereignty and independence of other states. Whether it is an individual person or a great world power, looking out for one's self derives virtue only by the avoidance of extremes. Neither a selfless abandonment of the reasonable interests of security and self-defense nor a selfish aggrandizement conforms to the conditions of living in the modern world. At its best the national interest implies, therefore, a respect for the rights and interests of others. President Eisenhower once remarked that he liked to think of national interest as "enlightened self-interest." How much risk to its national interest of security an enlightened nation should be willing to accept in deference to the interests and welfare of other states is one of those questions for which no simple rule of conduct can be stated.

To serve the reasonable interests of the nation with due respect for those of others should then be the objective of foreign policy; and inevitably, for nations as for individuals, self-preservation must be the most absorbing interest. Lord Palmerston's assertion well over a century ago that Britain "has no eternal friends, no eternal enemies, only eternal interests" holds today for any nation wishing to live. *Izvestia* once informed its readers that "the Soviet government bases its policy on its own interests."

Secretary of State Hull said as much for the United States during World War II, and other secretaries have done so too.

Interests have significant advantages as policy objectives. Unlike ethical principles, they can be negotiated and compromised without offense to the conscience or intelligence of diplomats and citizens. They are concrete and usually identifiable, whereas ethical principles are usually obscure and controversial. They provide a realistic base for policy because the interests of national security and welfare are the primary concern, the raison d'être, of all governments.

Finley Peter Dunne's *Mr. Dooley at His Best* records that in response to Mr. Hennessy's quick solution to the Philippine problem in 1899, Mr. Dooley noted, "An yet 'tis not more than two months since ye larned whether they were islands or canned goods." Then, after a lengthy discourse to Hennessy about the Philippines and their internal conditions and people, Dooley continued, "I larned all this fr'm th' papers, and I know 'tis sthraight. An' yet, Hinnissy, I dinnaw what to do about th' Ph'lippeens. An' I'm all aone in th' wurruld. Ivrybody else has made up his mind. Ye ask anny con-ductor on the Ar-rchy Road, an' he'll tell ye." This spoof on democracy at work, seeking a solution to a tough problem, is a sardonic comment on the information and skill exhibited in discussions of foreign policy.

Professor Charles Lerche expresses the same idea more directly: "Perhaps the most far-reaching, and the most difficult to contradict, of the asserted weaknesses of American opinion is its uninformed character." Although, as he says, Americans probably have better access to information than any other people, "the stark fact remains that mass audiences do not take advantage of the available data to the extent that one might expect."

Especially concerned that men skilled in some other field of intellectual effort feel qualified to make pronouncements on foreign policy, former policy maker Dean Acheson, to quote him once more, made the following statement in an October, 1969, interview:

> What also made me sick was the scientists' feeling that by making a bomb they knew everything there was to know about foreign relations, and could bring peace to the world. . . .
>
> The intellectual, strictly channeled into one discipline, wants to run them all. This is why Dr. (Benjamin) Spock gives me a pain, why Bill Coffin (Yale chaplain William Sloane Coffin) —a hell of a nice fellow—by being a Protestant clergyman knows everything about international affairs. He doesn't.

The contrast between the information of the people and that available to the chief executive has been pointed up by men who have been presidents. Both former President Truman and former President Eisenhower responded to questions from newsmen about foreign policies by saying that they no longer felt qualified to give an opinion, for they were without the sources of information available to the president—reports of the Central Intelligence Agency, the information gathered in the Department of State, and the wisdom of expert advisers. Theodore Sorensen after leaving Washington gave a similar reply to a question put to him on current policy. When, after he had vacated the vice-presidency in 1969, Mr. Humphrey was asked on "Meet the Press" whether he thought that the United States needed reconnaissance planes off the coast of North Korea, he replied that since leaving the government he had not had intelligence reports and was therefore unable to form an opinion.

Like Mr. Dooley, we of the public rely largely on newspapers for our knowledge, and we read them casually and often inaccurately. One of the most searching critics of democracy in the nineteenth century, Sir Henry Maine, based his opposition to the growing demands for popular government on the people's ignorance. The virtues of democracy, of popular participation in government, have proved to be so great, however, that Maine's rejection of it now appears mistaken; he might more wisely have seen in the limited knowledge of the people a reason for limiting their role and for achieving between them and their elected government a relationship which would combine a popular base at the bottom with knowledge and skill at the top.

One hundred and eighty years of foreign policy making in the United States have revealed the limitations of the people in contrast to the skill of the president. To be sure, both the people and the president have erred in judgment, but the batting average of the latter has been well above that of the former. Because there is no agreement in foreign affairs on what constitutes a base hit, this generalization cannot be supported by exact percentages. Whether President Johnson, for instance, should be credited with a base hit for his dispatch of marines to the Dominican Republic in 1966 is still a debated question. Even historians, with a better perspective on the past than contemporary commentators have on the present, often differ on the merits of an earlier policy.

Granting the lack of a formula for exactness, most of us, looking back into the past, would be inclined to uphold presidential policies over the contentions of their opponents, both in the "great debates" and in the lesser altercations. The wisdom of the early presidents in keeping the nation out of Europe's wars up to 1812 over the demands of large elements of the populace is now obvious. Today it is clear that when the war hawks finally took the nation into the war of 1812, President Madison's preference for peace and his hesitation to fight reflected a sounder concept of American interests than that prevailing in Congress and in the country.

The defiance by President Monroe and Secretary of State John Quincy Adams in 1818 of a clamor for the recognition of the new Latin American states so that a treaty with Spain for the purchase of East Florida might first be concluded now appears to have been wise. From today's perspective, Jefferson's purchase of Louisiana in 1803 and Seward's acquisition of Alaska in 1867 were sound transactions, although both were opposed by many well-meaning Americans; and it seems a mistake that the Virgin Islands were not bought in 1867, as Secretary Seward advocated, rather than in 1917 at an inflated price. Few Americans now denounce Polk's acquisition of thousands of square miles of land from Mexico in 1848 over an unimpressive opposition, and anyone advocating their return would be ridiculed. The pressure which the people exerted in 1898 on a reluctant president to go to war with Spain now appears hasty and ill-advised. President Wilson today stands higher in the esteem of Americans for his effort to take us into the League of Nations than do his opponents who kept us out. Subsequent events have shown that President Roosevelt assessed the international situation in the late 1930s more accurately than most Americans, that he was aware of the danger of war in Europe and of its implications to this nation's well-being, and that his proposals for a "quarantine" of aggressors and for a provision in the neutrality statute allowing him to discriminate in wartime trade against them were more realistic than were the neutrality laws enacted by Congress in response to public demands. Realizing more quickly than the people that a cold war was under way, President Truman took timely measures—rearmament, aid to Greece and Turkey, and negotiation of the NATO Treaty—which encountered a substantial opposition from elements of the public.

Like all human beings the president is quite capable of making mistakes. His opinion should be challenged, but with constructive intent and in a manner that meets the best rather than the worst traditions of democracy. What the 180 years of American national life demonstrate is that the advantages of the president in policy are meaningful and that dissenters should think at least twice before throwing hastily contrived obstacles in his way. The dissenter, in behalf of his own ethical and intellectual integrity as well as for the sake of sound policies, needs humility in addition to a sure source of information and a good store of wisdom. This is even truer now than when Washington, Adams, and Jefferson were president, for today's chief executive has available more resources by far for decision making.

The limitations of the people do not prove that democracy is unsound, nor do they show that the people should keep out of foreign policy. What they bring out is that in a healthy democracy the public should expect to play a less assertive role in foreign affairs than in domestic, and a less assertive role than they are now in the habit of playing. Foreign policy making, probably more than any other government activity, requires a high competence; yet it is the field in which the people are least able to be competent. This is no slur on the people; their deficiency is one that the citizens of all nations are born with and can never outgrow. Even the president himself, once he has left office, rejoined the populace, and become occupied with other interests, cannot be far ahead of the rest of the educated elite in his foreign-policy skill. The advantages which the chief executive has inhere in his office as much as or more than in his person.

Having in mind their limitations, what precisely can the people do and what can they wisely leave to their government in order to maintain a foreign policy of high quality and thereby advance their own interests? The answer depends upon the concept of democracy held by the person who gives it. The prevailing concept of democracy produces the confused foreign policy we now have. A more workable concept could produce a stronger policy behind which we could live more securely.

6. A Viable Democracy

ALTHOUGH DEFINITIONS of democracy vary, the idea of rule by the people may be clearly identified as the least common denominator among those formulated in the Western World. The English jurist Blackstone thought that a democracy exists "where the right of making laws resides in the people at large." To James Bryce it was "a form of government in which the ruling power of the state is legally vested, not in any particular class or classes, but in the members of the community as a whole." Professor J. A. Corry, in his *Elements of Democratic Government* (1951), explained it as "not merely a set of rules by which the people are governed; it is also a device by which the people govern their rulers."

When this general idea of rule by the people is translated into specifics by any several persons, diverse opinions on the essentials of democracy emerge. Concepts vary of who the people are and how they proceed to rule. Are the people all the male population except the slaves, as in Athens? Are they adult males only or do they also include women, as in the United States since 1920? Should adults be defined as persons over eighteen or persons over twenty-one? Are they literate persons only or do they also include illiterates? Once "the people" has been defined, does their rule require that they vote directly on all proposed laws or policies, or is it enough that the people elect their government and delegate to it the entire job of legislating and policy making? Or should they feel free, after they have elected a government, then to direct its activities in some detail? If so, ought the people to be satisfied merely to express opinions on how things should be done and to criticize, or should they exert pressure and coercion in order to have their way?

The American concept defines the electorate broadly. The suffrage legislation of the several states extends the vote to all adults over twenty-one years of age (but in two states the age requirement is eighteen, in one, nineteen, and in one, twenty); the considerable interest in fixing the age at eighteen may soon enlarge the electorate further. Residence requirements exist in all the states and literacy tests are required in a few. To quarrel with the idea of universal suffrage in one form or another would be foolhardy. If the people are to govern, all are entitled to equality in their basic rights and privileges.

The problems of the American democracy do not emanate from the size of the electorate but from the size of the task which it tries to perform, for the new democracy of present-day America holds not only that the people elect their government but also that they direct its work with expressions of opinion, with unrestrained criticism, with pressures, and with coercive demonstrations. No people have committed themselves to a heavier job.

American democracy is at least consistent, for it contends that the people are equal to any undertaking. This high estimate of the people is in large measure a legacy from Andrew Jackson. He maintained that any man is about as well equipped as any other to hold office and make political decisions; good common sense, in his mind, took precedence over special ability or experience. "The duties of all public officers," he argued, "are, or at least admit of being made, so plain and simple that men of intelligence may readily qualify themselves for their performance." This concept of democracy has by no means lost ground since Jackson's day; on the contrary, it has gained. American democrats are of all things self-confident.

The belief that nothing is beyond the capability of the people tends to produce a feeling that the more they do or try to do, the more numerous their contacts with policy problems, the more genuine is their democracy. The test of the new democracy is therefore quantitative, not qualitative, its vitality measured by how many people assert themselves on the largest number of points, rather than how well or wisely they cause the government to function.

The distrust of government mentioned earlier has also been a conspicuous part of the democratic equipment of Americans from the beginning, and no doubt it is in some degree present in people everywhere. Colonial Americans developed it from their unhappy experiences with the governors delegated by the British monarch to rule them. It was apparent in the provisions of the first state constitutions, written during the Revolution, designed to secure the people's liberties against governmental encroachment, as well as in the federal Constitution of 1787. Thomas Jefferson's democratic theory looked on government with suspicion and advocated as little of it as possible; his faith was in the common man. Andrew Jackson, too, taught Americans to distrust government and to believe in themselves. With his philosophy, it is understandable that he should advocate rotation in office, short terms, and strict limitations on reeligibility; long terms for officials, he preached, lead to "feelings unfavorable to the discharge of their public duties."

Another attitude of Americans which affects their conduct in government is their exaltation of the freedoms guaranteed in the First Amendment to the Constitution as basic to democracy: freedom of speech, religion, and the press, and freedom to assemble and to petition the government. These guarantees must indeed be regarded as an essential part of any democracy. Nothing about them, except the manner in which they may be and have been used, could be questioned. Circumspection in the manner in which the American people assert their opinions to their decision-making officials was once an accepted characteristic of their democracy. The point has been made earlier that the new democracy has changed all this. Now an end considered to be worthy is widely regarded as justification for the employment of any, or almost any, means.

Nowhere has the prevailing concept of democracy been more evident than in foreign affairs. Many people, especially since World War I, have shunned no task, no issue of policy. They have seen little reason to defer to experience, temperament, proximity to information, and time for deliberation. To impose their opinions upon the public and the government, they have employed methods oblivious of reason and pernicious to an orderly society. Minority protesters have claimed free speech for themselves but denied it to others.

The traditional American distrust of government has been carried further in foreign affairs during recent decades than ever before. Diplomats, generally rated low in the esteem of citizens, have drawn special fire from a suspicious public. Too many Americans would agree with the statement by an entertainer to our troops in World War II: "I wish that every diplomat could spend a day or two at the fighting fronts—and this mess would soon be over." Will Rogers's saying that "the United States has never lost a war or won a peace" voices a similar estimate of diplomats. Most telling of all, however, have been the attacks by the people on their secretaries of state, the nation's chief diplomats, throughout the cold war. Secretaries Acheson, Dulles, and Rusk were maligned, pictured as warmongers and evil-minded men.

The prevailing attitude toward secrecy in our dealings with other nations also reflects our democracy's distrust of public officials. When in 1955 a summit conference was scheduled at Geneva to deal with world problems, columnists and commentators speculated on whether another "Yalta" was about to take place; President Eisenhower was thrown on the defensive when it became known that he would speak for the nation at the conference. Regardless of the merits of the secret clauses in the Yalta Agreement of 1945, it is as true now as when de Tocqueville so contended in 1835 that every government must at times be able to bargain secretly and to make agreements that cannot be fully disclosed if it is to maneuver effectively against foreign foes.

No intelligence agency is regarded by the people whose interest it is designed to serve with more suspicion than the Central Intelligence Agency. In some measure this attitude has been engendered by the agency's mistakes in Cuba in 1962, by the disclosure of the mission of the U-2 brought down from the skies by Russia in 1960, and by unsubstantiated allegations regarding its activities abroad. Basically, however, the low esteem in which it is held by Americans is a reflection of their abhorrence of espionage (which constitutes a small part of the activities of the CIA) and their suspicion of any operation of the government which is not carried out in the open. They are ready to believe the worst about the CIA, as they did in 1967 when it was learned that the agency had given financial support to student organizations in international meetings and to labor unions, although no scandal had been disclosed. What is overlooked by the public in its attitude toward the CIA is its close bearing on the nation's security. Without its findings we would not have known about the Russian missiles going into Cuba, about the Russian development of a defense system against the missiles of the West, or about the missile strength of potential enemies.

No Americans have exhibited more distrust of their officials than the supporters of Senator John Bricker's proposal in the early 1950s to curtail by an amendment to the Constitution the power of the president to make treaties and executive agreements.

The proposal grew out of a fear not only that the president might abuse the power to negotiate treaties and agreements but also that two-thirds of the Senate might slip up and let a treaty impinging on our basic rights get by. Senator Bricker contended that "the American people want to make certain that no treaty or executive agreement will be effective to deny or abridge their fundamental rights." The extent of the popular distrust which it reflected is apparent from the fact that it had a substantial backing by congressmen, the American Bar Association, and many prominent citizens. Something irrational and unhealthy hides behind the extremes of distrust which Americans have exhibited. In effect it is a distrust of the democracy they profess to admire.

When he was an official in the Department of State, Carl Rowan told an audience of students, "A difficult thing for our open society, with its checks and balances, is the fact that while congressmen and editors and housewives and college students never pretended to overrule an Eisenhower or Omar Bradley [in military strategy], these groups eagerly declare their shrewdness in the field of diplomacy." The public does, indeed, usually desist from telling generals how to deploy troops or where and when to attack; recently, to be sure, laymen have urged the president, as commander-in-chief, not to bomb North Vietnam and not to employ napalm, have suggested that our troops be contained in enclaves, and have criticized the attack on Hamburger Hill. But these exceptions do not contradict Mr. Rowan's generalization that whereas the people see the need for expertness in military strategy and tactics, they will rarely concede that the strategy and tactics of diplomacy and foreign policy require an equal amount of specialized skill. Now more than ever the opinions and moral concepts of the people are uncertain foundations for policy moves.

Now the complexities of the process of foreign policy making are more baffling than when John Quincy Adams and President

Monroe formulated the Monroe Doctrine, and even then the decision to enunciate such a policy was complicated by alluring alternatives which had to be considered and eliminated. Now there are 125 or more states in the world, most of them affected in one way or another by American policies, as compared with 35 or 40 back in 1823, none of which could be injured or helped as much by what we might have done as can any of today's states. In the old days our relations abroad were mainly with the states of Western Europe, whose ways and culture we shared and understood; today we deal with Moslem, Buddhist, and Hindu nations as well as Christian, with blacks and Orientals and whites, with literate and illiterate, with well-to-do nations and poor, with democracies and dictatorships, and with capitalist, socialist, and Communist states, all of whom puzzle us with ways of life alien to our own.

Once foreign affairs was a leisurely profession in which public officials could take their time; but the world of today, in its scientific harness, rushes along with more speed than direction, producing the crises and near-crises that greet us daily in the morning newspaper. That the military power which has always lurked in the background of foreign policies has completely outgrown its old, familiar garments and donned a nuclear attire is a fact which must be uppermost in the mind of every American policy maker. Never before has the United States encountered anything in its policy planning as treacherous as the international Communist movement, which spawns aggressions easily and often. Almost as challenging is the revolution going on in the new underdeveloped countries aimed toward modernization and attainment of decent living conditions, a revolution complicated by the efforts of the Communist countries to capture its leadership.

In this threatening climate of international relations, policy makers, with a watchful eye on everything that happens, must spot each event and situation in which the United States has an interest and determine whether that interest is great enough to require action. If so—and in these days little of importance can happen abroad that does not affect us—they must set in motion the government's machinery for deliberation, assembling data and holding conferences and consultations, all of which will be kept at a minimum when action is urgent. In these deliberations they will be aware that while their latitude of action is theoretically broad, actually they are restricted by the hard facts of life. Aware that foreign and domestic policies are closely related, they will, if possible, devise the course least injurious to domestic policies and to the economy at home. They must explore the nation's capability to pursue and support contemplated courses of action; it would, for instance, be beyond the economic power of the United States to commit 80 percent of its production to the aid of needy nations, and probably beyond its military capability to conquer and govern an enormous nation like mainland China. Capability varies among nations. A nation like Nicaragua could not support any foreign-aid program worth mentioning; Britain is able to carry on a modest program but could not spend for that purpose two or three billion dollars per year, as does the United States. Were a policy maker to compute the cost of a course of action inaccurately, he could bring the country to disaster.

In devising foreign policies, a government often faces dilemmas. What it would do in one corner of the world may upset what it is trying to do in another; when the United States supports independence movements in Angola and Mozambique, it weakens NATO by alienating Portugal, trying to hold on to her colonies. Situations in which no conceivable action will be wholly constructive without at the same time causing harmful side effects abound. No policy for meeting the Communist threat in Southeast Asia has been discovered which would not be expensive to us in money, men, or both and bring down on our heads the condemnation of many nations; yet to do nothing could turn out to be expensive, too, and stir up criticism for our inaction. The

61

problem is like that of a physician who has no remedy which will not cause side effects quite as injurious to the patient as the disease itself; about all he can do in such a situation is nothing, letting his patient suffer, or experiment and take a chance on the outcome.

Rarely does the government face major issues of policy where the answers are simple, obvious, and sure. At the outset the policy maker may find himself perplexed about whether the national interest in a situation is vital enough to justify any considerable response by the United States: well-informed persons disagreed in 1965–69 over whether American interests in Vietnam were sufficient to warrant sending hundreds of thousands of troops there; our government, to the dismay of many Americans, decided that keeping South Vietnam free from Communist control was vital to the security of the free world. Then, when an interest is earmarked as substantial enough to require action, the policy maker must decide what his objective will be, how he would alter a situation abroad inimical to the nation's welfare. Again the answer may be debatable: In South Vietnam did we want (1) to keep the Communists out to the extent that the Viet Cong could have no part in the government, (2) to eliminate only North Vietnam from the affairs of the South and give the Viet Cong a share in the government, (3) to eliminate Communism from North Vietnam, as well as from the South, or (4) merely to preserve the independence of the South and leave it to the people there to decide their own future? At first it seemed that the objective of our government was the first of the four alternatives, but later number four was announced by Washington as the objective it sought.

Once an objective has been determined, a policy has to be formulated which gives reasonable promise of attaining it, for a foreign policy is only a means to an end, an instrument for accomplishing a fixed purpose. In Vietnam we first tried economic and military aid to the government of the South. When this proved inadequate, advisers were sent, and finally the armed forces were dispatched. Policy making is, then, a special process of reasoning, thinking through alternative courses of action and selecting the one likely to achieve the end in view most effectively and economically. It is clearly a process better utilized by a few informed officials than by the less well informed masses.

Much more than the general public, the president and his advisers are aware that a foreign policy is an instrument of only limited utility. It contains no magic but is a human instrument with very human limitations. It can do many things, but always at an expense of some kind and usually with less than perfect results. Unless the United States is willing to coerce other nations, it must be satisfied with efforts to influence them, efforts which, however well calculated, may prove futile. Tough international problems are the result of the actions of other nations as much as if not more than of our own, so that corrective measures on our side alone can rarely go more than halfway toward achieving solutions. As Justice Holmes once said, there are problems about which all that a person can do is to exclaim, "Well, I'll be damned!" Americans must live with the fact that they cannot match their industrial miracles with diplomatic miracles. In 1949, Secretary of State Acheson brought out the limitations of the policy maker as follows:

> One of my colleagues remarked of Americans in foreign affairs, that there is a general belief that anyone may put a nickel in us and we must come up with a policy to solve any probem. To think this oversimplifies the problems and completely misunderstands our role in world affairs.
>
> We can greatly help those who are doing their utmost to succeed by their own efforts. We cannot direct or control; we cannot make a world, as God did, out of chaos. There are some, apparently, who think we should do this, and in less than 6 days.

Competent writers have for some time been directing attention to the tendency in this country toward a reshuffling of the powers of government away from the traditional balance between the executive and legislative branches and to the advantage of the former. This was brought out in Professor James Burns's recent book, *Presidential Leadership*. In an article published in *Current* (April, 1965), Professor Hans Morgenthau emphasized the ways in which scientists and experts, with their esoteric knowledge of public problems, have brought about an "extension of executive discretion."

Inevitably there is a tendency in all organizations, public and private, for decision making to drift toward those most knowledgeable in the subject matter at hand. Knowledge is indeed power, and whatever form it takes, power of some kind will prevail. When presidents have dominated policy to the dismay of Congress, it is because, with their staffs of experts both in and out of the administrative departments, they can think with the help of a larger fund of information than can the men on Capitol Hill. Instead of lamenting the tendency for the control of foreign policy to center in the president's office, we might well applaud it. To try to stop it by public demonstrations and wholesale opposition is to place artificial barriers in the way of a healthy urge in this democracy to utilize skill, barriers unnecessary for the preservation of democracy so long as the chief executive utilizing the skill may be held accountable to the people through the election process.

In foreign affairs the drafters of the Constitution intended that the president would play a dominant role and for that reason gave him almost complete control over diplomacy, the initiative in treaty making, a legal basis for concluding executive agreements, and command of the armed forces. In recent years, as foreign policy has come to involve esoteric knowledge possessed mainly by experts in economics, law, diplomacy, government, history, science, and military affairs, the wisdom of the constitutional provisions placing the chief executive at the center of the foreign-policy process is more apparent than ever. Such experts can be made available to him, but they cannot be provided to the 535 members of the Congress, either individually or collectively, with an expectation of equally constructive consequences. Suggestions have been made that the Senate Foreign Relations Committee have a larger staff of specialists, and this might be helpful, but the advisory function loses much of its intimacy and relevance when directed toward a group.

The availability of experts to the president cannot, of course, diminish his responsibility, nor does it imply the "eclipse of personal judgment" referred to by Hans Morgenthau; the chief executive can be counted on to merge the advice received with his own considered judgment and his assessment of public thinking, which no one near him can, as a rule, match on a national basis. He is no robot, but a man of wisdom, usually great wisdom. As such, he uses advice as he pleases, accepting or rejecting it. He decides between conflicting advice, with which he is constantly confronted. But he is always free to do what he pleases, as President Lincoln brought out in a widely publicized cabinet meeting where, after all of his cabinet had voted "no" on a proposal under discussion, he announced that the "ayes" (he alone had voted "aye") had it. What the advisers do for the president is to provide him with facts, data, and alternative courses of action. He is but one of many in deliberations, but in decision making he stands alone.

How is all this related to the people or to the democracy which they profess? It does not mean that American democracy tends to become less real, but it does signify that it has been struggling to become more effective, to gain in the quality of its policy decisions. It imposes on the people the need to think of democracy in a different way, to respond with approval to the president's urge to be a more effective center of decision making in foreign policy, rather than with vituperation and insinuations that he seeks the destruction of democracy. It demands a realization that government by the people can be improved by better processes which will give this country a fair chance to deal with profound problems abroad while at the same time retaining popular sovereignty. It is an affirmation of the statement by Adlai Stevenson when he was campaigning in 1948 for the governorship of Illinois: "I think the efficiency, the simple honesty—the quality in short—of government by the people must improve all along the line: at the city level, at the state level, as well as at the national . . . if it is ever going to hold our own faith and respect." It is a rejection of the pessimistic view that efficiency and democracy are antithetical.

A democracy of quality which is trying against heavy odds to establish itself will see in the president not a man bent on deceiving and defrauding the people but one as committed to their ideals and aspirations as any person in the nation. The statement is commonplace but often forgotten that the office tends to stimulate in the men who hold it an almost superhuman effort and devotion to the public interest. It has transformed mediocre men into great men and great men into legends. When Harry Truman became president after the death of President Roosevelt, so little was expected of him that many observers remarked that both political parties should take more pains to nominate capable men as candidates for the vice-presidency; but his record in office now entitles him to the high place that he holds in the esteem of the nation and in the annals of history. Some presidents have been weaker or less effective than others, but the general average has been high enough to justify the implication of one of the subheadings in Professor Burns's book: "Why Great Men Are Chosen Presidents." In office, a president is aware that he has nowhere higher to go except into the history books.

Paradoxically, among the components of a healthy public attitude toward all government officials within a democracy, both confidence and suspicion deserve a high rating. Without public confidence, officials are afraid to commit themselves to decisive policies, and when they do so their policies will be subjected to indiscriminate mutilation. Without suspicion, officialdom becomes careless both in its morals and in its efficiency. The trick is to maintain the two components in the right proportion. Today the American public, especially in foreign affairs, runs too high in suspicion and too low in confidence. A presumption in favor of a presidential foreign policy rather than against it would not be a dangerous concession to tyranny. The acceptance of secrecy in foreign affairs where the president deems it advisable, without accusations of traitorous maneuvering or charges by the press that their "right" to information has been violated, would not require an inordinate amount of confidence.

A mistaken notion persists that the president stands for dictatorship, the Congress for democracy. This is strange logic, for both were chosen by the people and both may be rejected in the next election. Indeed more people vote for the president than for any other official, and presidential elections elicit more interest, thought, and discussion than those for any other official or group of officials. Moreover, the chief executive is, as a rule, more capable than individual members of Congress of sensing public thinking on a national basis, and he will defy it with great reluctance and only when, in his opinion, the nation's welfare demands that he do so. Then, too, as Walter Lippmann has pointed out, when the president makes a decision, it is not "as it was in 1823, by private consultation among a few leading men." Thus it has come about that although a person may disagree with his president, he cannot reasonably reject White House policies as inherently undemocratic.

The concept of democracy which the times demand and, indeed, are forcing upon us will also require that the people be less in the foreground of foreign policy. It will recognize that the degree of democracy prevailing is not proportionate to the level of the activity of the people in foreign affairs. To the contrary, by trying to do too much the people may end up by doing nothing, or at least doing nothing well. The advocates of the short ballot a few decades ago used to point out that the long ballots encountered by voters at the polls, listing the names of candidates for the electoral college (or the president), the Senate, the House of Representatives, state legislatures, governors, state offices, county and city offices, together with a group of preferred legislative proposals, cause unintelligent or blind voting. The electorate is not governing when the burden imposed upon it is so heavy that it cannot know the relative merits of the hundreds of candidates on the ballot or of the half-dozen or more referred measures. In foreign affairs, too, democracy becomes a travesty when the people undertake to do more than they are equipped to do, when they reduce the president to a machine converting into action what they, or what those among them who can exert the greatest pressure or make the most noise, dictate.

As James Reston once observed, the traditional theory of American government is that the people know best. This doctrine, still very much alive, holds that there resides within the people, at least within a majority of them, some occult power to find the right answers to all questions. During the long years when our needs in foreign policy were minimal we got along on this dubious assumption tolerably well. But now that our continued existence in freedom lives behind a foreign policy that must outsmart crafty enemies while avoiding a final world war, one's faith in the instinctive rightness of the people no longer remains unbounded. Mr. Reston was right in saying, "Personally, I do not believe that the constitutional assumption that 'the people know best' is a very reliable guide to the conduct of American foreign policy today." We are, as he went on to say, engaged in an underground war, an economic war, and an intelligence war; in cold-war conflict, intuition as a guide to policy is surely as hazardous to democracy as it was to the irrational Adolph Hitler.

Whether or not democracy can work in the precarious field of foreign policy depends in the final analysis on the kind of democracy you are talking about. If a democracy embodies the current American concept in which the people assume to be better equipped than their president to fix policies; look with excessive distrust on their elected government, especially the president; and fail to distinguish between activities and conduct appropriate to domestic affairs and those appropriate to foreign affairs, then de Tocqueville, Bryce, and other skeptics were right—it will fail in foreign affairs. If the democracy is one in which the people are aware of their soverign position but not intoxicated with the resulting power, are informed of their limitations and schooled to live within them, are conscious of the advantages of a dynamic leadership and of a cooperative public, its foreign policies will prosper.

7. What the People Can and Cannot Do

WITHOUT SELF-ANALYSIS, democracy becomes disoriented, unreasoned, and unreasonable, as do other forms of government and all other human agencies. Only a conscious effort can prevent its governing bodies, as intricate in their own way as the parts of a computer, from getting out of balance and unreliable. Because American democracy has never been keen on self-analysis, it is already out of balance and sterile in its conduct of foreign affairs; we have what Walter Lippmann in his *Public Philosophy* has called "a devitalization of the governing power" and a "derangement in the relation between the mass of the people and the government." Because the people are pushing aside the government and trying to do more in policy making than they can do well, they are devouring their democracy; in the name of democracy they are destroying democracy.

What are the capabilities of the people in foreign affairs? They vary, of course, with some individuals more interested and better equipped than others. The mass public, the total adult population of the country, drugged by apathy, has a low level of ability to analyze policy problems. As some one has said, it is a sleeping giant, happily unconcerned with public problems most of the time, but when aroused, able to wield tremendous power; a Pearl Harbor will transform it into a force to be reckoned with.

The so-called alert public, composed of those people who are interested enough to inform and express themselves on current issues, are the makers of the public opinion to which the government must answer in its policy moves. To all intents and purposes it is "the people."

The collective IQ of this alert public cannot be ascertained in figures. In foreign-policy competence its individual members range all the way from those whose knowledge has been gleaned from quick glances at the headline news to the occasional men and women with substantial backgrounds in reading, travel, journalism, teaching, foreign trade, or membership in societies interested in public affairs, such as the League of Women Voters. The precise size of the alert public varies; it is larger and more assertive on security issues like Vietnam, smaller and less boisterous on less vital issues such as the conclusion of a consular treaty with the Soviet Union. As vital policy issues have become more numerous since World War I, the total number of Americans composing the alert public from time to time has tended to increase, as noted in an earlier chapter. Circumstantial evidence suggests that they have become better informed as time has passed and have taken their job more seriously, perhaps too seriously. The irony is that as the alert public has been educating itself, policy problems have grown still more numerous and complex; the total result is another frustrating case of running fast to stand still.

In foreign affairs there are activities in which the alert public (the people) can engage with benefit to policies, and others which will almost certainly be injurious. The pages that follow elaborate on this point, but to begin with, several generalizations basic to sound policy making in a democracy are pertinent:

1. The people should recognize that direct action on policy projects, such as the referendum on certain treaties in Switzerland or the Bryan proposal for a referendum on a declaration of war, would be unwieldy in this country.

2. The people should concern themselves in policy matters primarily with objectives and purposes rather than the details of strategy and tactics.
3. The people should be in a position to know where decisions have been made and be able to hold the official or officials who made them responsible.
4. The people should be prepared to exercise self-restraint during the more critical periods of policy making.
5. The people should expect during crises that their government will ignore them more than usual, perhaps entirely, and give them less information.
6. The people should emphasize reason and persuasion in their methods of self-assertion.

As J. P. Warburg asserted in the title and contents of a book written in 1944, foreign policy begins at home. A State Department pamphlet a few years ago declared that foreign policy reflects "what we are and what we want." It is a "social process," according to Felix Gross, and therefore is largely controlled by the concepts and ideologies within the country—the political, economic, social, religious, and ethical assumptions prevailing among the people.

The significance of this fact is that without so much as uttering a word or raising a hand, let alone picketing the White House, the people have a great deal to say about American foreign policy. They fix the limits within which their government may operate, barbed-wire fences which it cannot safely hurdle. The president, a native-born citizen of the United States, has been brought up on American ideology and knows as well as anybody the fence hazards within the country. He knows the religious doctrines of the churches and their ethical tenets so well that, without the advice of the clergy, he has a clear idea of what we look upon as right or wrong. Even better than the church leaders, he is aware of the conflicts that can occur between ethical dogma and the requirements of national security, and the resulting dilemmas faced by the policy maker. He knows that Americans are generous and will endorse efforts to help the new, struggling nations. He might wisely guess, too, that economic or military aid to Yugoslavia, Poland, and other Communist nations would encounter the opposition of American upholders of capitalism. Whatever his own opinion on the matter, he would be aware that to begin a preventive war or to be the first to use nuclear weapons would be to entangle himself in the barbed-wire fence. Americans are, as the chief executive realizes, peace-minded and will go to great lengths to avoid a fight; they oppose policies of aggression by ourselves or by others. Fervently committed to democracy, they incline toward policies that discourage authoritarianism abroad and encourage nations striving for a government of the people.

It is both creditable and disconcerting that while agreeing almost unanimously on some ideological tenets, Americans differ vehemently on others. It is creditable in that it reflects democracy's guarantee of the right to think and to speak freely, but it is disconcerting to the policy maker who cannot be sure of how high the fence is in some places, or even whether any fence is there at all. This lack of unanimity characteristic of democracies was especially troublesome between the two world wars when the people were divided into isolationists and internationalists. Before 1914 Americans generally had made a fetish of isolationism so that it was virtually traitorous even to consider acting as though we were a part of the world, especially the European world; so strong was this commitment that when in 1906, President Theodore Roosevelt agreed to mediate at Algeciras in the Franco-German dispute over Morocco, he felt bound to explain that he was not forsaking the traditional doctrine. Then, after World War I, when American interests pointed to cooperation in world affairs, the habit of isolationism was so deep-seated that it could not be entirely shaken off. From 1919 to 1941, presidents found that the split between those Americans who held on to isolationism and those who gave it up was so profound that sensible policies were difficult or impossible on the League of Nations, the World Court, Japanese aggression in China, the Italian invasion of Ethiopia, the Spanish civil conflict, the Nazi threat, and the war that broke out in 1939.

Since World War II, Americans have disagreed on another basic ideological issue—the role of power, particularly military power, in foreign policy. Earlier generations passed on to us a low estimate of the military side of life and a disdain for power politics. Charles Lerche states the point well: "As a nation whose history has been 'the vindication of Puritan morality,' it was strictly in character for the American people to reject power politics on grounds of immorality." We have preferred the legalistic-moralistic approach to international problems. This refusal of Americans to dirty their hands with the instruments of power politics was one of the props supporting isolationism.

The beginning of the cold war found the United States in a strange new position in the world, a position we would have preferred not to occupy: we were the only nation with enough power to contain Communist aggression. The choice our government had to make was to renounce power politics and let Russia take all of Europe and perhaps other free nations, or to rearm and place our power between the Communists and the free world. President Truman, after the Eastern European states had been made into Russian satellites, decided on the latter course and began to build up the armed forces, make alliances, and extend economic and military aid to nations in peril.

Although our nation as a whole was not ideologically prepared for this turn of events away from its secure past into the vortex of power politics, many Americans saw the necessity for the turnabout and backed the government. Others, including pacifists, near-pacifists, neoisolationists, and some of the church leaders, held back, regarding themselves as the government's loyal opposition. This ideological split on the question of power in international relations remains today, somewhat accentuated by an emotional fervor that has built up on both sides. Presidents devising policies for Southeast Asia, NATO, Berlin, the Dominican Republic, the Congo, and other areas have been in the unenviable position of being damned if they do and damned if they don't use the nation's power to contain Communist expansion.

By annihilating the opposition, distorting the truth, and imposing censorship, dictators can secure ideological unity, or at least a semblance of it, for policy making; the Nazis and the Communists have done this mercilessly and effectively. But among democracy's virtues is a tolerance of ideological diversity. Our government uses nothing more potent than persuasion to influence public thinking on such subjects as isolationism or the use of power in the Dominican Republic, Vietnam, or elsewhere; it tries to justify its actions in speeches, news conferences, and State Department publications. The public has the democratic option of accepting or rejecting what the government tells it.

Where the people are divided on a fundamental question, as they were on isolationism and internationalism and as they now are on the use of power, the inevitable result is an internal struggle to control government policies. This places the government in the dilemma of not knowing what it can count on. A foreign policy of strength is impossible. The decision maker is paralyzed. He is responsible to the people, but the people do not know what they want, or they want conflicting things.

What American democracy needs most of all at the present time is a healthy philosophy of foreign policy in which power, especially military power, is given its due, no more and no less. The tendency of many people is to write off power completely as too hideous for a civilized people; the idea of using any kind of power—physical power most of all—to have one's way is anathema to them. The basic issue here is whether the Western World can eschew the military while its enemy, the Communists, will use it whenever it suits their purpose and they dare. Aware of the widespread rejection of military power in the West, the Communists often dare to take chances with us, as in Korea, Cuba, Vietnam, and Berlin. Our greater reluctance to use force and their awareness of that reluctance mean that our policy wins less respect from them than theirs does from us.

Americans are familiar with the place of power in domestic politics—the power of trade unions, the farmers, the blacks, the Democratic party, the Republican party, and others; nothing, indeed, can be done in politics without power in some form to work with—votes, threats of withdrawal of support, money, appeals to the people, or personal influence. The domestic politics of some countries utilizes power in the form of force, as in nations where military leaders employ the army to attain office, a practice well known in Latin America. The Guatemalan mother who, in answer to a query about what profession her son was going into, said he had "bought a gun and was going into politics," understood the role that force can play even in domestic politics. Americans learned the same unhappy fact in the Civil War. The difference between politics among sovereign states and politics within them is that the former, less sophisticated than the latter in most parts of the world, places greater emphasis on the military as a form of power.

As power in some form is an essential ingredient of all politics, so is it a vital part of any nation's foreign policy. The purpose of a foreign policy is to do something—to get what is desired, to keep what is already possessed, or to effect a beneficial change where it is needed. Such objectives cannot be achieved merely by wishing for them or even by asking for them, any more than a political party can elect a president simply by wanting to.

Much has been said during the last half century about the need for the people to become better informed in order to be more effective in international affairs. Usually this is intended to mean that they should read the papers and periodicals with greater avidity and go to more meetings where they will hear talks on Vietnam, foreign aid, or the United Nations. Desirable as these activities may be, they fall short of the requirements of an active citizen.

The people are handicapped in their thinking on world problems not so much by a lack of information on current issues—although they are handicapped in this respect—but rather by their lack of a well-considered philosophy of international politics. They read the papers without the ideological tenets, background knowledge, and assumptions necessary to transform facts, rumors, events, and allegations into tenable opinions on policy problems. Without a guiding philosophy, the thinking of the people tends to be shallow. The quality of public thinking would be enhanced by a greater understanding of the fundamentals of international politics—the place of power; the nature of Communism, nationalism, and imperialism; and problems of economic development. That such subjects sound dry and forbidding does not diminish their relevance to the foreign policies that intrigue Americans. More sophistication in the ideological foundations of policy could hardly be expected to produce a unanimity of attitudes, but it could at least enable people to disagree with each other or the government more intelligently. If by chance a few holes in the fence were plugged up, that little would be a help to the policy maker and to the quality of American policy.

Free elections are democracy's most effective safeguard. As long as they persist and are conscientiously employed, the government belongs to the people. The right to hire and fire, implicit in the right to elect, is reliable insurance against dictatorship. So profound are its consequences that, as noted earlier, a habit of distrusting elected officials must be regarded either as pathological or as evidence of the people's distrust of themselves and of democracy. And to the extent that elected officials are not worthy of confidence, the people have failed in their principal job. Should the electorate make a mistake, they will have an opportunity to change their government at the next election; from the people's point of view, elections are periodic audits, and audits are vitally important. In his *Considerations on Representative Government,* John Stuart Mill wrote, "Men . . . do not need political rights in order that they may govern, but in order that they may not be misgoverned."

Important as they are to democracy's foreign affairs, national elections are not referendums on specific issues, nor do they provide clear mandates for the president to follow in decision making. Never in American history has a presidential or congressional election revolved entirely about some one foreign-policy question. Every election is loaded with issues, foreign and domestic. Until recently, domestic issues—slavery, prosperity, cheap money, farm problems, and labor—dominated, and sometimes nothing seemed more important than a feeling that "it is time for a change." Issues of foreign policy were important in American politics in the 1790s; the Texas and Oregon problems were prominent in the election of Polk in 1844; imperialism was one of several subjects of debate in the election of 1900; and in 1920 there was much talk about the League of Nations, although most analysts have agreed that the return to Harding's "normalcy" was uppermost in the minds of voters. But at best foreign-policy issues are so entwined with domestic that what the electorate's views are on any one can never be clear. Democracy's guns, at least its election guns, are not so constructed as to be able to hit on target dozens of issues separately, although they can blast at a collective group, whether in 1800, 1920, or 1968, with awesome effects. What the electorate can and does do at the polls is to register its satisfaction or dissatisfaction with the administration's total accomplishment, as against the hopes offered by the opposition party.

Often in a given election the two major parties are not far apart in the foreign-affairs portion of their respective platforms or in the programs advocated by their respective candidates. This was true, for instance, in the presidential election of 1960. At first Kennedy and Nixon seemed to clash on the question of defending the islands of Quemoy and Matsu against the mainland Chinese, but later both came to agree with the Eisenhower policy of defending the islands if necessary to guarantee the security of Taiwan or the Pescadores. Both candidates were against nuclear testing in the atmosphere, but Kennedy thought that one last effort for a treaty with Russia on the subject should be attempted. On policies involving Cuba, foreign aid, Africa, and Latin America, differences between the two leaders were not discernible. In the election of 1964, candidates Goldwater and Johnson appeared to differ sharply on policy in Vietnam, with the former supporting the tougher line, but when the election was over, Johnson's policy turned out to be very like that which his opponent had proposed; moreover, the Vietnamese issue in 1964 was but one of many—social security, government spending, the future of the TVA, military preparedness, and others.

In the congressional elections of 1966, the question of Vietnam was given some attention by candidates, but political experts agreed that in no state except Oregon did it have first place in the debate. Inflation, the war on poverty, government spending, and hosts of local issues dominated. The points of view of the many candidates over the country were so diverse on Vietnam that to construe the final outcome as significant to that problem was impossible: a few candidates wanted to get out of the country soon; some emphasized negotiations; some favored President

Johnson's policy; and others advocated applying all the force needed to defeat the Communists quickly. Asked at a news conference just before the election whether he thought the results would show a public will on Vietnam, President Johnson answered in the negative. After the election, a few observers, Mr. Nixon in particular, thought they saw in it a popular desire for a tougher line, but most analysts were of the opinion that it disclosed nothing significant. Editorial comment often took the view that the election was a demand to slow down the "great society."

Whether there was significance in the fact that in 1968 the two most dovish aspirants for nomination at the Democratic Convention, Senators McCarthy and McGovern, failed, is not clear. In any case, Vice-President Humphrey, whose position on Vietnam was assumed to be about the same as that of President Johnson, was nominated. In the campaign which followed, Nixon for the Republicans pledged an early end to the war but did not explain how he would end it or what kind of peace terms he would seek. A meaningful clash on Vietnam did not emerge between the two parties either in their platforms or in the campaign; Nixon seemed to feel that he had the election won and that, as president, he would have a freer hand without precise commitments, whereas Humphrey appeared unwilling to deviate far from Johnson's policy even though in his own mind he may not have agreed with it entirely. And once again a multiplicity of issues, foreign and domestic—Latin America, foreign aid, inflation, the balance of trade, poverty programs, law and order, the continuance of the surtax, and the plight of the cities—complicated the chances of finding a mandate on foreign affairs or anything else. Apparently the people wanted a change, but the direction they wished it to take was blurred, especially in foreign affairs.

Even were it possible to discern a popular mandate on foreign policy in a given election, it could mean little in the changing international scene. In the election of 1916, both Wilson and Hughes went on record for a continuation of American neutrality in World War I, and the slogan "He kept us out of war" was loudly proclaimed in Wilson's favor; but on April 2, 1917, the president went before the Congress to request a declaration of war. Both Roosevelt and Willkie pledged in the 1940 campaign that American troops would not be sent to Europe, but in 1942 they were on their way. Had Presidents Wilson and Roosevelt not shifted their policies with the altered international situations they faced, the American public would in all probability have been enraged, for it, too, had drifted into a harder line toward the aggressors. Not only did the people fail to hold the presidents to their pledges, but most Americans were actually pleased that their chief executives acted as they did.

Regardless of talk about bipartisanship in foreign affairs, the two political parties have felt free to debate policy issues during election campaigns; efforts to avoid contention in behalf of a strong policy have been fruitless. Looking forward to the election campaign of 1956, Secretary of State Dulles issued the following warning:

> Foreign policy will no doubt be debated during the Presidential campaign. Such debate should be welcomed so long as it is con- structive and conducted in such a manner as not to endanger our nation. It needs to be remembered that those hostile to the United States and its ideals are not going to take a vacation so that we here can safely concentrate on a domestic political battle.

Similarly, President Johnson in May, 1968, warned presidential aspirants of the danger to current policy efforts that might result from open debate. He appealed to them to avoid misleading the enemy about who "speaks for the United States" and asked them not to court publicity with uninformed criticism. He asked the nation to "size up the man" who speaks freely without full information. Inevitably, whether warned or not, candidates are unable to resist the temptation that foreign-policy charges and countercharges seem to offer for political gain. In 1956 the candidates freely debated nuclear testing, Suez, the Middle East, and other problems. Four years later, in the 1960 election, politics took precedence over policy needs when candidates Kennedy and Nixon debated Kennedy's allegation that the Republicans had allowed a "missile gap" to develop so that Russia was ahead of us. Candidate Goldwater challenged administration policies in Vietnam in 1964, advocating a tougher line. Again in the election of 1968, Vietnam was fair game for candidates both in the primaries and in the election.

In view of the fact that elections do not furnish mandates on foreign policy or bind newly elected or reelected presidents to earlier policy statements, debates on foreign policy in campaigns can have no considerable utility except to win votes. A danger they present is that allegations against the policies of the administration may prompt the candidate representing it to rebut the charges with facts and data which should not be disclosed; Nixon must have been tempted to produce figures with sources on the "missile gap" in 1960, but evidently either he or the president believed such a course would be unwise. A public debate also runs the risk of instilling in other nations a contempt for an administration policy that seems weakly supported at home. Despite any logic that might be advanced against capitalizing on foreign-policy issues in campaigns, especially during the cold war, political man is so constituted that he is not likely to stop his politics at the water's edge. What might reasonably be asked of campaigning parties and candidates is that they use restraint in their charges and countercharges relating to foreign affairs. For a politician to grab what democracy has to offer—freedom to speak freely in campaigns—without acknowledging the duty it imposes—self-restraint in behalf of the national interest—cheats the constitutional system under which he lives.

Although, as Carl Becker has said, "democracy is a kind of Gladstone bag which, with a little manipulation, can be made to accommodate almost any collection of social facts," no one outside authoritarian regimes would exclude from its contents the freedom to criticize the government. Democracy gives the platform even to those who would annihilate it. Its self-confidence is such that it believes that in a free exchange of ideas it will survive, stronger than ever. The benefits of opposition are acknowledged both in the British House of Commons and in the American Congress by according a special status to leaders of the opposition party.

The right to speak and write freely, on which the freedom to criticize is founded, is not unlimited in the American democracy. As Judge Oliver Wendell Holmes's oft-quoted observation in *Schenck* v. *United States* (1919) pointed out, "The most stringent protection of free speech would not protect a man in falsely shouting fire in a theatre and causing a panic." Neither will free speech shelter libelous statements by one person against another. Even the right to speak freely on public questions has been severely curtailed in times of national emergency like war, as in the Sedition Act of 1918 and in sections of the Alien Registration Act of 1940. The Supreme Court has several times tangled with the problem of where a reasonable line may be drawn between the duty of the nation to protect public safety and the right of the individual to dissent. In the case just cited, Justice Holmes stated the "clear and present danger" doctrine, to the effect that limitations on the individual's freedom are justified "when the words used are used in such circumstances and are of such a nature as to create a clear and present danger." The Court would have the final word in a given situation on whether the danger is such as to justify a limitation of the right to dissent.

Except when the United States is in a declared war and restrictions have been imposed by statute, Americans have felt no compunction in speaking out freely on issues of policy, even in times of serious national emergency. As noted before, this was true in the critical years of the 1790s when the government was trying with difficulty to pursue a policy of neutrality toward the European war then going on. It was true throughout the troublesome 1930s when the Nazis, Fascists, and Japanese were taking long chances with the peace and the Spanish Civil War was straining the diplomatic skill of the government in Washington. Most extreme of all has been the loud criticism by millions of Americans of the undeclared war in Vietnam, directed both against the war itself and against the manner in which it has been fought.

The public demonstrations of dissent which the new democracy has introduced into American politics have raised unanswered questions of how far the constitutional rights of free speech and assembly may be carried. Critics of policy who parade in large numbers on public streets, picket, display threatening or insulting signs, hold sit-ins, or occupy public buildings maintain that their conduct is protected both by the Constitution and by accepted principles of democracy. The demonstrators at Chicago during the Democratic Convention of 1968 assembled, so sympathizers assert, with peaceful intent to let the country, the government, and the Democratic party know their opposition to the war in Vietnam and their desire for peace. Since a man or a crowd may speak their criticism of policy, the argument runs, by conduct as well as by words, a public demonstration is a form of free speech protected by the First Amendment to the Constitution. Supporters of such demonstrations would remind us of the proverb that "actions speak louder than words."

Justice Black of the Supreme Court was interviewed by Eric Severeid on this question of free speech. The justice refused to comment on the Chicago affair, presumably because cases relating to it might come before the Court. But on the general question of whether demonstrators are protected by the First Amendment to the Constitution, he thought the answer was negative. He said that the First Amendment "protects speech. And it protects writing. And it protects assembly. But it doesn't have anything in it that protects a man's right to walk around and around and around my house, if he wants to; fasten my family up into the house, make them afraid to go out of doors." He asserted that it is not true that "the only way to protest anything is to go out and do it in the streets"; he mentioned other ways—by elections, through political parties, and in certain forms of assembly. It is by no means clear that the full Court would agree with Justice Black, but if it did, public demonstrators would find it difficult to conform legally to the American style of democracy.

Some of the state courts have had occasion to rule on the limits of the rights of free speech and assembly. On May 10, 1969, the Kentucky Court of Appeals handed down a unanimous ruling involving student protesters who, in defiance of an order issued by the University of Kentucky, held a sit-in within its buildings in protest against job-recruiting efforts of the Defense Intelligence Agency on the campus. The court held that the rights of free speech and assembly do not "insulate" student protesters from the legal consequences of their actions. The prohibition by university officials of the use of campus property for such a purpose was, in the opinion of the court, a proper exercise of their duties as custodians of property and as agents of tax-paying citizens. Students entering buildings when they had been told to stay out were trespassers. The court declared that "the right of free speech, of assembly, or of petition, does not carry with it a passport to exercise it in a place where the person who would exercise it knows full well that he has no right or license to be." The opinon also asserted that the existence of a constitutional right is "neither a sword to cut up the rights of others nor a shield against the consequences of conduct that otherwise violates the law." Whether a ruling of this kind would stand in the United States Supreme Court is not clear. But that there are limits to the rights of free speech and assembly binding on dissenters is quite probable.

Although demonstrations appear to be an accepted method of dissent within the new democracy, they are indeed hard to square with sound democratic doctrine as the Western World knows it. At its best, democracy is presumed to emphasize reason, not the emotionalism of the crowd, to give differing views a forum for public airing and debate in order that wisdom may prevail. Demonstrations may emphasize a point of view but they do not substantiate it. They advertise without giving evidence of the merits of the product. The product may be meritorious—and certainly this has been true in the civil rights movement—but in foreign affairs the likelihood is less, for the issues here are not a matter of ethics alone, and they are further removed from the ken of the man on the street. In any case, demonstrations on issues of domestic policy are always less dangerous to the nation's security than those in the delicate field of foreign affairs, where enemies watch closely for signs of American vacillation.

A public demonstration is primarily a tool of a minority. A majority has little need to get out in the street unless to counter the noise of a minority; to President Nixon, it is "the great silent majority." In a democracy political minorities must have tools of some kind to avoid what James Bryce called the "tyranny of the majority." And, he argued, a majority is tyrannical "when it decides without hearing the minority, when it suppresses fair and temperate criticism of its own acts, when it insists on restraining men in matters where restraint is not required by the common interest, when it forces men to contribute money to objects which they disapprove and which the common interest does not demand, when it subjects to social penalties persons who disagree from it in matters not vital to the common welfare." Such acts of wantonness he did not find characteristic of the United States when he wrote his *Democracy in America* (1913), nor do they exist today. The precious rights of minorities have been protected not only by the constitutional rights of free speech and assembly but also by a spirit of fair play that has pervaded American life in the past.

86

Public demonstrations tend to upset the balance that has hitherto obtained between the majority and the minority; here, as at so many points, a democracy derives its good health from balance. The demonstrator confronts American politics with such a challenge to the majority that the present danger is a tyranny of the minority. His methods of self-assertion contain an element of coercion against the government (usually supported by the majority). The power of the mob, harnessed by a minority, can be terrifying to all who read about it, see it on television, or witness it in person. To government officials it is intimidating, suggesting open rebellion unless demands are met, and often posing a problem of whether the police or the national guard should be called in; state governors and city mayors know that they are on the spot. Demonstrators do not need to carry guns to frighten the people or the government. The coercion is more subtle, if a mob can be said to be capable of subtlety; it is the coercion of angry faces, hostile placards, and insulting cries against assumed enemies. Whether the cause of the demonstrators is good or bad—and it may be a good one—their methods are based on a precarious concept of democracy.

Dissent as practiced in the United States in this era of the new democracy is poison to a healthy foreign policy. A policy under attack at home cannot be taken seriously abroad. And if the policy is one related to national security, the American style of dissent may be fatal. Dissenters against Vietnam policy have been loath to admit that their conduct has encouraged Ho Chi Minh, weakened the American effort, or prolonged hostilities. Professor Arthur Schlesinger, Jr., went to some length in 1967 to explain that critics and demonstrators had not injured the war effort, saying, "The evidence suggests that our adversaries are fighting not because they expect us to collapse but because they believe fanatically in their own cause." He maintained, "The proposition that dissent in America is losing the war in Vietnam is, on existing evidence, much less a fact than an alibi" for the

87

failure of a policy. He did not submit any of the evidence he referred to in these two statements.

Evidence has been available to prove that the Communists have indeed been encouraged by dovish opponents of presidential policy. American journalists in Hong Kong have reported this to be true. It was also disclosed in an editorial in *Nhan Dan* (November, 1966—at the time of the congressional elections), labeling the American critics of the president their own "second front." The editorial further asserted that "the Vietnamese people highly value the protest movement of the American people against the war in Vietnam." The reader is told that "the struggle of peace-loving Americans" was causing "serious headache and fear" to the White House and the Pentagon. For the North Vietnamese not to be encouraged by American weakness on the home front would be manifestly stupid on their part. News in 1918 that German morale was buckling lifted Allied hopes and strengthened the determination to fight on.

Public officials in the United States have hesitated to condemn dissenters for injury to their policies in Vietnam, no doubt because to do so might be interpreted as an attack on the tradition of free speech. Timidly at first and later quite bluntly they expressed themselves. Averill Harriman, one of the first to voice the government's frustration, said in 1965, "The longer it will take to convince critics that the United States is right in South Vietnam, the longer it will take to convince the Communists that they cannot win." In reply to a question asked sometime later on a national television program about whether his department was embarrassed by the furor at home, Secretary Rusk said, "Well, I think there are those abroad who lean heavily on those speeches [of critics]." Still later he warned that while the right of dissent is basic to "a thriving democracy such as ours," the dissenters were obstructing the chances for peace in Vietnam by misleading "the other side" into believing that this country "is wavering in its purpose."

President Johnson denounced with increasing impatience those Americans who had lashed out against his policy in Vietnam. At first his statements were restrained, merely noting the "false picture" of American determination which the debate in this country was giving to the Asian Communists. After the popular demonstrations of October, 1965, in our cities and colleges, both he and the State Department made a special effort to deny the claims being made in China and Russia that protesting Americans were more representative of our thinking than was the government. When he returned in early November, 1966, from his trip to Southeast Asia, the president made a plea for unity behind the nation's policy. In a later press conference he denounced those critics who were demanding a cessation of American bombing in North Vietnam, and asked why it was that they appealed only to one side to moderate hostilities rather than to both.

On December 12, 1967, President Johnson spoke to the AFL-CIO convention, a friendly audience which had just adopted a resolution in support of his Vietnam policy. As though he had finally found a friend, he made the following points:

> I am very proud and gratified, Mr. Meany, for the resolution you have passed here in support of freedom's cause. . . . I thank you for another man. He does not live in the White House. He does not guide the destiny of the nation and he doesn't have the responsibilities throughout the world on his shoulders alone. But he is face down in the mud of the D.M.Z. He is out there storming a hill near Danang. . . . The American soldier thanks you from the bottom of his heart. . . . I wish that those who bewail the war would bring us just one workable solution to end the war. The peacemakers are all out there in the field. The soldiers and statesmen need and welcome the sincere and responsible assistance of concerned Americans. But they need reason more than they need emotions. They must have a practical solution and not a concoction

of wishful thinking and false hopes, however well intentioned and well meaning they may be.

On November 13, 1966, a group of 139 prominent Americans, many of whom had had close contact with public affairs, came out with a signed statement that failure to draw a line between responsible and irresponsible criticism of American policy in Vietnam would encourage Communists to delay peace negotiations. Among the signers were former President Eisenhower, former Secretary of State Acheson, Senator Jacob Javits, Dr. James Conant (former High Commissioner to West Germany), former Undersecretary of State Robert Murphy, and former Postmaster General James Farley. The statement drew attention to several "fantasies" which irresponsible critics had circulated:

1. That the war is "Lyndon Johnson's war, McNamara's war, or any other individual's war."
2. That American leaders are "committing war crimes or indulging in genocide . . . ."
3. That this is a "race war of white versus colored people . . . .
4. That our leaders have "a compulsion to play 'world policeman' or to conduct some 'holy war' against the legitimate demands of underdeveloped peoples."

Still concerned with the effect dissenters were having on American policy, some of the men who had signed the 1966 statement, along with former President Truman, Lucius Clay, and others, late in 1967 organized a Citizens' Committee for Peace with Freedom in Vietnam. They stated that "voices of dissent have received attention far out of proportion to their actual numbers." The objective of the new organization, they asserted, was "to make sure that Peking and Hanoi will not mistake the strident voices of some dissenters for American discouragement and a weakening of will."

President Nixon's peace negotiators in Paris have been hurt, too, by the vacillation on their home front as the Communists have pressed for maximum concessions from the United States. Statements in 1969 by Ambassador Thuy to Ambassador Lodge revealed an awareness of the impatience of many Americans for a quick settlement regardless of the cost. It is understandable that when President Nixon presented his peace proposals to the public on May 14, 1969, he urged the people to unite behind the project in the interests of a peaceful solution to the war. Several times later, notably in his address to the people on November 3, 1969, he pleaded for unity in support of his work for peace. Two days before the peace moratorium of October 15, 1969, Secretary of State Rogers said that in his opinion Hanoi's reluctance to begin negotiating seriously was caused by its feeling that the president would not have "the support that's necessary to carry on for a long time." With his usual forthrightness, Vice-President Agnew lashed out at the "impudent snobs" who were undermining the president's policy; significantly, President Nixon a few days later praised Agnew for the "great job" he was doing as vice-president.

Hanoi's stake in the cause of the public protester came out unmistakably just a day or two before the peace moratorium of October 15, 1969, when Premier Pham Van Dong wrote a letter which was circularized in Paris and read on the radio in Vietnam, wishing success to "the United States' progressive people" and demanding that President Nixon "put an end to the Vietnam aggressive war and bring all American troops home." The premier expressed his conviction that the common cause in the "struggle of the Vietnamese people and progressive American people against the United States' aggression will be completely successful."

The temper of public criticism reflects the prevailing concept of democracy in the nation. Because the American people are inclined to think of democracy as indifference to skill in decision making, as distrust of elected officials, as unlimited participation by the people in government, as an abandonment of self-discipline, and as mob demonstrations, much of the criticism is acrimonious, unrestrained, and irresponsible.

Methods of criticism and dissent cannot be safely based on an assumption that what democracy permits it approves, any more than personal conduct can be founded on the theory that whatever the law allows is necessarily acceptable to society. Democracy's justification of itself is its high estimate of the individual person—his integrity, his worth, and his good judgment. It assumes that what it permits the people will do only if the nation will not be injured. It admits the possibility that the people will fail to foresee a potential injury to the nation or that they will be indifferent to it. But democracy—and for that matter every form of government—is in large measure a gamble, the ultimate payoff of which depends on somebody's wisdom and integrity. The earmark of democracy is that the bet is by the people on their own wisdom and integrity, not by a group of Nazis or Communists on a dictator.

What are reasonable restraints on criticism? In the first place, a democratic people would be tactically sound and prudent to pack whatever criticism and debate they have to offer into the period during which the government is considering policy, before a final decision has been made public. At this stage of the policy-making process, popular opposition will be less frustrating and embarrassing to the government than later, after a decision has been put into force. The "great debate" of 1919–20 over the League of Nations at least had the merit that it occurred when, under our Constitution, the treaties of peace were still before the government awaiting Senate approval. The only injury to policy making of reasoned dissent before a final decision would be delay, the seriousness of which would depend upon the circumstances. Where a situation calls for quick action, as in the 1965 revolt in the Dominican Republic, the government must be expected to act without waiting for a public debate. The people might appropriately have debated the Vietnam problem in the early sixties, but at that time, and in keeping with the limitations of the public, we, unlike the government, were not even aware of an emerging problem.

Once the government has announced a policy decision or given it effect, criticism made publicly is, by intent, destructive; it is an effort to defeat or at least to modify a course of action already in operation. This will not be too harmful if the policy at stake bears only slightly on the national interest. It could be tolerated, although it would be somewhat embarrassing to the government, on our cultural exchange policy; it would be somewhat more serious but probably not out of place if the policy were foreign aid. But where criticism is leveled at an existing policy immediately concerned with security and already involving force, a threat of force, or even a possibility that force may be used, public criticism and debate are surely a deliberate attempt to sabotage the considered effort by the president to protect the nation against an enemy, as serious as though a declared war were in progress.

If dissenters from an existing policy with security implications feel impelled to express their opposition, they would be prudent to limit their methods to confidential communications addressed to appropriate government officials. This was the recommendation of former President Eisenhower, whose experiences with critics had been somewhat less harrowing than those of Presidents Johnson and Nixon. Speaking of the Vietnam debate, he said, "I have constantly said (and shall continue to say) that, first, there is only one spokesman for America in conducting our foreign affairs." After approving President Johnson's stand against the Communists in Vietnam, he continued, "To this I add that if there is anyone who opposes the President in his conduct of foreign affairs, he should send his views on a confidential basis to the administration; none of us should try to divide the support that citizens owe to their head of state in critical international situations."

Fear by a policy maker of intemperate criticism, like the criticism itself, emasculates policy. Working for a people who are habitually irresponsible, the president must be as intent on finding a policy that will avoid trouble to himself as on devising one that is sound. Remembering President Johnson's trials, President Nixon on assuming office could hardly be blamed for what appeared to be an ultracautious attitude designed not to stir up either the doves or the hawks while working for peace in Vietnam. Fearful of the public, a chief executive might prefer inaction to action as long as he can get away with such a course. At least two roads lead to paralysis in policy: executive fear to act decisively and an irresponsible popular challenge to a policy.

The President's fear of indiscriminate dissension is also a temptation to act in secret or at least to withhold full information on actions which he believes need to be taken but which may set off a violent public reaction. No doubt the secret clauses in the Yalta Agreement were partially inspired by the fear on the part of Roosevelt, Stalin, and Churchill of public furor, not only in the United States but elsewhere. Presidents Johnson and Nixon considered the Communist penetration of Laos to be a matter of concern to the United States and through the medium of the CIA provided the Laotian government with military advice and air support. The operation was not as "clandestine" as it was alleged to be, for it was often in the daily news, but it was not brought officially to the attention of Congress or the people. It eventually annoyed the Senate Foreign Relations Committee to the point that in October, 1969, that body opened hearings on it.

Public opinion reaches decision makers by many routes. Traditionally Americans have felt free to send letters, telegrams, or petitions to the president, secretary of state, and other officials dealing with foreign policy. Each week from one thousand to five thousand personally written letters are received in the Department of State. A special staff analyzes them, categorizes their contents, and makes the results available to interested officials. To repeat, this is a constructive democratic procedure even for a policy already in operation, for it lets the government know what people are concerned about without a public free-for-all and without the publicity either at home or abroad that advertises disunity or weakens policy. The procedure informs without attacking; it affects policy without embarrassing the government in the eyes of other governments and peoples. Public officials often acknowledge the benefit which they derive from such contacts.

Organized groups of people interested in foreign affairs, like individuals, have ways of getting the ear of the government, some of which are well within the limits of mature democratic action. Sending, without publicity, petitions and resolutions to government officials is a practice which a democracy will encourage. Testimony before congressional committees on policy in the making can also be constructive, but, naturally, the spokesmen representing groups with a close relationship to a given problem are heard with more interest than others; the National Federation of American Shipping would be listened to eagerly on a policy involving ocean transport, and the American Trade Association's point of view on the renewal of the Reciprocal Trade Agreements Act would carry weight. Organizations close to a problem, by the very nature of the interests they represent, can lobby with congressmen or the president effectively and without public excitement or furor.

Although public officials profess the highest respect for the communications that reach them, they would not be expected by a sophisticated citizenry simply to count the mail and vote accordingly. Better is it for officials to decide against the majority view if there are good reasons for doing so. As Edmund

Burke said to the people in 1774, "Your representative owes you, not his industry only, but his judgment; and he betrays instead of serving you if he sacrifices it to your opinion."

No group has entered foreign-policy debates with better motives than the churches. The kind of world they seek is the kind that most Americans desire. Yet spokesmen of groups whose outlook in foreign policy is basically ethical or emotional prove more confusing than helpful to decision makers. An organization like the National Council of Churches speaks to a policy only from the ethical point of view, and because the ethics of any policy problem such as Vietnam or the Dominican Republic are debatable, it cannot be authoritative even in its own area of interest. Then, too, the National Council of Churches cannot speak for the millions of its unconsulted church members, but only for the few leaders who formulate its pronouncements. What is most objectionable in its methods and in those of student, pacifist, and near-pacifist groups is that they are not retsricted merely to conveying points of view to the government but in effect constitute public attacks on policies to which the government is committed. They draw no distinction in their public acts between policy in the making and policy already adopted by the government and in operation. They aim, not to avoid embarrassing or handicapping government policy, but rather to arouse opposition, domestic and foreign. They attack the government as vigorously when it is in the midst of an international crisis as in periods of calm.

Thomas Bailey in *The Man in the Street* remarks, "If religion is important to us, and if foreign policy is also important to us, each is bound to have some effect on the other, for the two cannot be compartmented in our thinking." This profound truth suggests that the churches' main area of operation in foreign policy must be the body politic, to provide it with a leaven of Christianity which will affect all thinking within it. The church's job in politics is to make good people, the sine qua non of a sound democracy; to make good policies is the job of the government. In his First Epistle to the Corinthians, St. Paul wrote as follows:

> For the body is not one member, but many. If the foot shall say, Because I am not the hand, I am not of the body; is it therefore not of the body? And if the ear shall say, Because I am not the eye, I am not of the body, is it therefore not of the body?

St. Paul might have been talking of the body politic and used much the same logic, for it, too, is made up of many "members": the government, the churches, the farmers, the factories, the railroads, the electorate, and the school. Each has its own work to do, and the work of each is essential to all the others. The churches, the electorate, and the schools, by doing well their respective tasks, strengthen the government in all its activities, including foreign policy making, but none can do the work of the government. The work of the church is fundamental; in a way it is the heart, pumping life through the entire body politic. It has no cause to say, "Because I am not the government, therefore I am not of the body."

One danger of the churches is that their incursion into policy making renders them less effective as makers of good people. Gallup surveys of American opinion in 1957 and 1968 on the question, Should the churches keep out of political and social matters—or should they express their views on day-to-day social and political questions? were revealing. In 1957, 44 percent of the people wanted to keep out, but in 1968, 53 percent took this position. An article in *Trans-Action* (June, 1968) by Rodney Stark and Charles Glock, entitled "Will Ethics Be the Death of Christianity?," noted that "the long Christian quest to save the world through individual salvation has shifted to the quest to reform society." This, they believed, was responsible in part for the church's diminished appeal to the people. Again, its most effective method of reforming society might be to reform more millions of individual Americans.

A church position on a question of foreign policy, and on other political issues as well, must be a dogmatic one; promulgated as God's will, it must be absolute and final. Consequently, a person who honestly differs with the church is confused, if not alienated. He begins to doubt whether church leaders can be authoritative in their own field if they stray (as he believes) in lay subjects. In any case, he joins a church not to learn about foreign policy but to learn about God; he has ample opportunity to hear about politics elsewhere.

The reconciliation of democracy and foreign policy demands self-disciplined news media which inform without giving away security secrets and which express views on policy in the making without attacking security policies already in force, thus splitting the public during a crisis. Without an ingrained sense of self-restraint the journalist finds himself in an unending war with his government. Information that makes exciting news will not necessarily make for strong policies.

Press, television, and radio discussions of policy in the making and during declared wars have usually been consistent with the requirements of sound, democratic policy making. Most reporters are, as former President Eisenhower said of the Washington press corps, "men of stature." But in times of crisis short of a declared war, the self-restraint which foreign policy needs has been lacking. Speaking to the members of the Bureau of Advertising of the American Newspapers Association in April, 1961, right after Castro's adversaries in this country were defeated in their effort to land at the Bay of Pigs, President Kennedy made the following appeal to the press for self-discipline in the cold war:

> But I do ask every publisher, every editor and every newsman
> in the nation to reexamine his own standards, and to recognize the

nature of our country's peril. In time of war, the Government and the press have customarily joined in an effort, based largely on self-discipline, to prevent unauthorized disclosures to the enemy. In times of clear and present danger, the courts have held that even the privileged rights of the First Amendment must yield to the public's need for national security.

Today no war has been declared—and however fierce the struggle may be, it may never be declared in the traditional fashion. Our way of life is under attack. Those who make themselves our enemy are advancing around the globe. The survival of our friends is in danger. And yet no war has been declared, no borders have been crossed by marching troops, no missiles have been fired.

If the press is awaiting a declaration of war before it imposes the self-discipline of combat conditions, then I can only say that no war ever posed a greater threat to our security. If you are awaiting a finding of "clear and present danger," then I can only say that the danger has never been more clear and its presence has never been more imminent.

In the same address the president reminded his hearers that "every democracy requires the necessary restraints of national security," but that he preferred self-imposed discipline over restrictive legislation. He noted with regret that "this nation's foes have openly boasted of acquiring through our newspapers information they would otherwise hire agents to acquire through theft, bribery, or espionage."

During the hostilities in Vietnam, the news media have been particularly careless. Editorials attempt to sabotage government policies, blacken the image of the military, and in other ways contribute to the unrestrained dissent of Americans. Television news reports show the horror of the killing on battlefields and in the streets, as though to stimulate popular opposition to the American effort by having the viewers actually see what everybody should know—that war is hell. The kind of self-discipline which President Kennedy asked for has been exercised by only a few reporters. In the name of democracy the major portion of the news media has committed itself to the destruction of democracy's policy.

Trying to maintain a foreign policy which the news media are bent on destroying is a frustrating job. President Washington condemned the "infamous papers" that opposed his policy of neutrality toward the war then going on in Europe. Lyndon Johnson unequivocally made known his annoyance at newsmen in their treatment of his policies. Recently, in November, 1969, Vice-President Agnew berated the television commentators and the journalists for what he believed to be their bias, especially in regard to Vietnam policy. Denouncing government censorship, he posed the question of whether the news media were not themselves censoring by their discriminatory selection of the news and opinions they present. He was particularly disturbed that right after President Nixon had pleaded for national unity to support his peace-making effort with the Communists, the networks had "trotted out" opponents of executive policy to promote disunity. Many Americans agreed with the vice-president. Even critics felt inclined to reexamine their positions.

Unofficial polls have become an accepted part of American democracy. George Gallup, Louis Harris, the National Analysts, the Opinion Research Corporation, and other pollsters sample public opinion and tell the people themselves, the government, and the world how Americans think on the issues of the day. Presidents watch the published findings with interest, both to see what the effect of the findings may be on their policies and to discover the degree of success they may have achieved in an effort to capture public support.

The polls have been unusually conspicuous in reporting opinions on the fighting in Vietnam. The total results of the findings of the pollsters, as analyzed by Seymour Lipset in *Trans-Action* (September–October, 1966), indicated up to that date considerably more backing than opposition to presidential policy. Respondents to questioners wanted peace and favored negotiations to that end but opposed getting out of South Vietnam in such a way that the Communists could gobble up the country. Strong majorities hoped that the United Nations would take over the problem from the United States, either to fight or to settle the issues behind the war. Most people upheld the president's policy of applying as little force as possible to attain the ends sought. Substantial minorities were found, however, in opposition to government policy: at one extreme those for leaving Vietnam forthwith regardless of the consequences, and at the other extreme those favoring a step-up in hostilities to gain a quick victory.

Since 1966 frequent polls on many phases of the government's Vietnam policy have been reported in the press, on the wisdom of the American presence in Southeast Asia, further escalation of hostilities, the proposal to confine American soldiers to enclaves, proposals for negotiations, and the cessation of bombing. They have shown a growing disenchantment with the war but general opposition to leaving Vietnam without an "honorable" peace.

Like the critics of foreign policy, the pollsters have not been inclined to heed the demands of an effective foreign policy when security interests have been at stake. Presumably they would not take the risk in the midst of a declared war of advertising to the world any minority or majority within the public opposed to it, although they might well publish polls on issues of a possible future peace settlement; the same risk is present in an undeclared war, such as that in Vietnam. It would be surprising if the Communists have not been pleased to learn the size of the president's opposition and to note that it has tended to increase. To advertise dissension on a policy in force which is designed to serve the nation's security is quite as harmful to the country as to create it. The pollster, like the critic, would be prudent to confine his reports to policies in the making and policies already adopted by

In Britain there is a personal tie between the executive and legislative branches which ensures cooperation: the prime minister and his cabinet are not only members of Parliament but also its official leadership. Because their party is the majority party in the House of Commons, they can count on a favorable vote for their policies and for whatever money may be requested. Those M.P.'s who belong to the prime minister's majority party will think twice before defeating government projects, not only because they know that their leader can dissolve the House and call for a new election, but also because they are unlikely in that election to have the party support they need. Party discipline in the House is so strong that for a member of the governing party to get out of line is hazardous to his political future. Only minority party members feel free to harass the government with adverse votes and criticism.

The American democracy is quite different, for the executive and legislative branches are completely separate; the president and his cabinet are not and cannot be members of the Congress and do not necessarily belong to the party in control of it. Even if the president's party has a majority in Congress, party discipline is so weak that defection is easy and frequent. A congressman, whatever his party allegiance, knows that he is free to defy the policies of the chief executive with little danger to his career; he may lose presidential patronage, but this he can live with. He has a guaranteed term of two or six years, so that the president cannot interrupt his tenure by springing an election. The total result is not only that executive leadership here is weaker than in Britain but also that legislative harassment of executive policies is greater.

Recognizing the essentially executive nature of the conduct of foreign relations, the Constitution lodged in the president all the power that he needs to carry on effectively, provided the Congress and the people do not check him unduly. The list of his powers is short but far-reaching. His right to appoint (with the consent of the Senate) and receive diplomatic representatives, together with that of negotiating treaties, gives him a complete monopoly over all communications with foreign governments. No other official, not even the Congress itself, can send to or receive from a foreign government any official delegate or message. The Supreme Court elaborated on this diplomatic power of the chief executive in *United States* v. *Curtiss-Wright Export Corporation* (1936). The Court quoted with approval John Marshall's statement of 1800 in the House of Representatives that "the President is the sole organ of the nation in its external relations." It asserted that "the President alone has the power to speak or listen as a representative of the nation," and that "into the field of negotiation the Senate cannot intrude; and the Congress itself is powerless to invade it."

This executive right to "speak and listen" for the United States reaches deeply into the area of policy making. Diplomacy, which speaking and listening add up to, is an arena for the enunciation of policies, perhaps to be later embodied in treaties. The foreign policy of President Theodore Roosevelt to build the Panama Canal was set forth in the diplomacy that led to the Hay-Pauncefote Treaty of 1903; the Truman-Acheson policy to contain Communist expansion in Western Europe was first negotiated with other governments and then inserted into the North Atlantic Treaty in 1949. Policies not successfully brought into treaty form are also continually asserted in diplomacy by the president's representatives. The American policy of arms limitation has been advanced by diplomats, without agreement, many times since World War II, in both bilateral and multilateral discussions.

Control over diplomacy also carries with it an opportunity to make and give effect to policy in executive agreements, some of which vie with eminent treaties in their bearing on the national interest. John Hay's open-door policy was incorporated into agreements in the form of notes exchanged between him, acting for President McKinley, and the representatives of other nations. The Yalta Agreement was concluded by President Franklin D. Roosevelt with Premier Stalin and Prime Minister Churchill during the course of conversations relating to wartime and postwar problems. If a subject can be treated in diplomacy, it can be dealt with by executive agreement, but if the subject is one that requires application within the country by the courts, the agreement must be supplemented by an act of Congress or given the status of a treaty in order that its provisions may become the law of the land. No doubt it is true, as senators have charged, that presidents have used executive agreements to evade the Senate in treaty making; when the Senate in 1905 refused to give Teddy Roosevelt a treaty with the Dominican Republic allowing the United States to collect customs in that country to pay off its external debts, he made an executive agreement to accomplish his purpose. Two years later the Senate gave its consent to a new treaty on the subject.

The Constitution further strengthens the president's hand in foreign policy making by its provision that "he shall from time to time give to the Congress information on the state of the Union, and recommend to their consideration such measures as he shall judge necessary and expedient." This provides him the best forum in the land for the announcement of a policy, aimed perhaps at a foreign as much as a domestic audience. Significant policies have been enunciated in this manner: the Monroe Doctrine (December 2, 1823), Wilson's Fourteen Points (January 8, 1918), Roosevelt's Four Freedoms (January 6, 1941), and Tuman's Point Four program (January 20, 1949). The president may also use other forums for this purpose, as did President Eisenhower when he announced his "Atomic Power for Peace" program before the General Assembly of the United Nations. Whenever he speaks, his hearers know that he is the only man who can "speak or listen" for the United States.

As commander-in-chief of the armed forces, the president possesses still another instrument for the enunciation of policy. The disposition of troops, fleets, or airplanes can loudly affirm an existing policy, and in appropriate situations may in itself proclaim a policy. President Polk's dispatch of troops in 1846 into territory claimed by Mexico conveyed a policy message that Mexico could not fail to hear. In 1908, President Theodore Roosevelt sent a fleet on a trip around the world to tell the Japanese that the United States had a policy of interest in the Far East.

The powers of the Congress in foreign policy are less positive than those of the president; they do not penetrate the areas where the action is. Used in support of presidential policy, they strengthen it impressively; employed negatively against policy, they weaken or perhaps destroy it. So crucial is the role of Congress that the reality of the separation of powers in foreign affairs stands out unmistakably.

The most far-reaching of all the powers of Congress is that of appropriating money to meet the needs of the nation in foreign affairs. This is a whip hand enabling Capitol Hill to do many things, even to be rash if it pleases. It can fix the size of such policy commitments as foreign aid and the Peace Corps; indeed, it can terminate both if it wishes to do so. The Congress can reduce the size of the Department of State, or starve it to death for want of funds, and there have been times when that department has been left uncomfortably hungry.

The power of the Congress to raise and maintain the armed forces permits it to give size and shape to the military instrument which the president will have behind him or may actually deploy in his policy moves. In the 1930s, as World War II was approaching over the horizon, the strength of the armed forces was not what President Roosevelt wanted and no doubt needed. In recent decades, with the world in turmoil, the chief executive, quite naturally, has been more sensitive than the Congress to the

107

need for a strong military arm in foreign affairs. Congressional debates on the antiballistic missile system requested by President Nixon (and approved by a small majority) is indicative of the negative influence, beneficial or not, which Congress is in a position to exert.

The statutes often necessary for policy, especially in the implementation of the special programs our government has carried on abroad since World War I, are also within the discretion of the Congress to give and shape or to withhold. The list is a long one, including the Trade Agreement Act (1934), the neutrality statutes (1935–39), the Lend-Lease Act (1941), the Greek-Turkish Aid Act (1947), the Act for a National Security Council (1947), the Interim Aid Act for Europe (1948), the Foreign Assistance Act for Europe (1948), the Mutual Security Act (1951), and many others. Such legislation both authorizes action and defines the limits within which the executive may move.

In the exercise of its legislative power in foreign affairs, the Congress has at times cramped the president in his policy efforts. In their foreign-aid programs, for instance, recent presidents have been obliged annually to settle for smaller appropriations than they believed essential. President Franklin Roosevelt in 1935 had to accept a neutrality law which rejected his plea for a right to discriminate against an aggressor in wartime trade. For the most part, however, the Congress has reacted conscientiously and quite favorably to executive requests for appropriations and for statutory authority to set up desired programs.

The special powers of the Senate in the field of foreign affairs are well known. The Constitutional Convention of 1787, aware that the several states were giving up their right of separate action in foreign affairs, deemed it expedient to associate the Senate, in which the states were to have equal representation, with the president in treaty making. And at the insistence of the southern states, a two-thirds rule for Senate approval was adopted, intended to protect them against a treaty depriving them of navigation rights on the Mississippi River, which they had feared for some years. The Constitution consequently stipulates that the president "shall have the power, by and with the advice and consent of the Senate, to make treaties, provided two-thirds of the Senators present concur." This provision has long been one of the most controversial in the Constitution. John Hay often voiced the frustration he felt with the Senate's conduct in treaty making, and in 1899 he blamed his ill health on the "minority of the Senate which brings to naught all the work a State Department can do." Occasionally movements have been launched to amend the Constitution so as to substitute both Houses of Congress acting by a simple majority vote for the two-thirds of the Senate in the approval of treaties, but all have died. Critics point to the inconsistency with democratic dogma of the present rule, which permits a decision by a minority over the majority. In practice, the Senate's part in treaty making has probably been less harmful to the nation than a theoretical analysis of its role might lead critics to expect, although the Senate has harassed many secretaries of state and presidents, notably Secretary Hay and President Wilson. The two-thirds rule has defeated some twenty-five treaty projects—not a large number, but among them were a few of special importance, such as the treaties of peace (1920), the St. Lawrence Waterway Treaty (1934), and the treaty for United States admission to the World Court (1935). The vast majority of those approved have been without reservations.

The other special function of the Senate in foreign affairs is to approve the appointment of "ambassadors, other public ministers, and consuls." The established practice of the Senate is to approve presidential nominees as a matter of course, although nominees are commonly interrogated in the Foreign Relations Committee. Better cooperation with the president in this particular could not be asked for.

The manner in which the Constitution divides the control of foreign affairs between the president and the Congress is an open invitation to both competition for dominance and to cooperation in the interest of a strong policy. Our history has witnessed much cooperation, but it is also replete with rivalry in which the Congress has sought the upper hand. Conflicts have more often been won by the president than by the Congress; the real loser, however, has usually been the nation. Like a dormant volcano, executive-legislative hostility can erupt at any time.

The power of Congress to appropriate money, potentially one of its most telling weapons of combat, is often so circumscribed by conditions created by the president that its cutting edge is dulled. This fact, irksome to a Congress that is jealous of its control of the purse, came out for the first time in 1796, when President Washington requested an appropriation to implement a commitment made by him in the Jay Treaty. To affirm its right of independent action, the House adopted a resolution asserting that it was the "right and duty" of the House to "deliberate on the expediency or inexpediency of carrying such Treaty into effect." Following this announcement that it felt free to do as it pleased, the Congress voted fifty-one to forty in favor of financial support for the unpopular Jay Treaty. Although members of the House have since affirmed and reaffirmed their independence in supplying funds to meet presidential commitments in treaties, they have always come through with the cash.

More irritating to the Congress have been executive deployments of troops abroad in time of peace in such a way as to require appropriations for their maintenance. When this happens the Congress has two options: to provide the funds needed for the support of the troops, or to leave them stranded. The latter would be so disastrous that it could not be seriously considered, and therefore the former becomes the only practical course of action. Thousands of troops in Vietnam cannot be left unsupported. Teddy Roosevelt sounded out the Congress to determine whether it would provide funds to send a fleet around the world. Finding no congressional interest in the project, he decided, so he said, to start the fleet on the trip anyway, sure that the Congress would make money available to bring it home.

The Congress, trying to reverse the handicaps, has occasionally taken the offensive against the executive with its financial power. At times it has pitted itself against the president's authority to "speak and listen" for the nation in diplomacy. In 1826, when President John Quincy Adams asked Congress for funds to finance a diplomatic mission to the Panama Conference, an attempt was made in the House to attach a rider to the appropriations bill, prescribing instructions to the delegation that would be sent. The argument was advanced that the power to make appropriations carries with it the right to impose conditions. In the House, Daniel Webster argued that the project would be an unconstitutional impairment of the president's control of diplomacy; after a debate the rider was dropped. In 1924, however, when the Congress appropriated money for the expenses of the American delegation to the Opium Conference, it did attach a rider specifying that the delegates might not sign an agreement unless a list of conditions were met; when it became clear that the conference would not agree to those conditions, the delegates withdrew.

A challenge to the president's right to deploy the armed forces abroad in time of peace was made in Congress in 1912, when the presence of American troops in Nicaragua was under criticism by leading senators. It was based on an assumption that the Congress, in appropriating funds for the army, could itemize the purposes for which the money might or might not be spent. Senator A. O. Bacon submitted an amendment to the army appropriations bill to the effect that the funds could not be used to transport, pay, or supply any part of the army "employed or stationed in any country or territory beyond the jurisdiction of the laws of the United States." After Senator Elihu Root objected that the amendment would encroach on the president's power as commander-in-chief, it was defeated. Since 1912 similar proposals for curbing the power of the president to send the armed forces abroad in time of peace have been made in Congress and defeated. Other methods, too, have been tried, but in vain. In practice the commander-in-chief has sent the armed forces abroad some 125 times without congressional authorization and in some instances over the opposition of prominent members of Congress. The president's power as commander-in-chief has proved to be as hard to curtail as that in diplomacy.

Its power to regulate foreign trade is another weapon which the Congress has tried to employ against presidential discretion in foreign affairs. An instance of this occurred in 1965 when Senator Karl Mundt and Representative Charles Halleck proposed to stipulate in the Trade Agreements Act then up for renewal that the president be denied the right to make trade agreements with Communist nations. Opponents of the proposal contended that it was an attempt to usurp the president's authority to conduct foreign relations. Walter Lippmann argued that if it were done, the chief executive would be "limited and stultified as is no other head of government in the non-Communist world." After some debate the Congress turned the proposal down.

The most available of all congressional weapons in the competition for policy control is the resolution. The joint resolution, one of several types of resolutions, is not adapted to influencing or coercing the president in policy matters or to usurping his powers. By its nature it must be approved by both houses of Congress and signed by the president (or passed over his veto), and obviously he will not sign any document pretending to establish a policy to which he objects.

Concurrent (by both houses of Congress) and simple (by one house) resolutions are the usual vehicles of congressional efforts in policy. The extent of their use is indicated by figures for the twenty-six years between 1925 and 1951, when a total of 1,164 were introduced, of which 202 were adopted. In purpose and content they may be friendly or unfriendly to the president. The Senate's Magdalena Bay Resolution in 1912 was in no way embarrassing to President Taft; its warning to Japan that no alien "corporation or association" might acquire any land in this hemisphere which could be used as a military base was an elaboration of the Monroe Doctrine quite agreeable to the chief executive.

More often than not, however, resolutions are intended to criticize, embarrass, or prod the president in policy situations. The recognition of new governments or states abroad has from time to time been the subject of such efforts. The Constitution has nothing specific to say about where the power to grant recognition is lodged, and like other unnamed functions, it has elicited keen rivalry. It has been generally conceded that from his right to send and receive diplomatic representatives, which is the essence of recognition, the chief executive has a clear title to the power. Members of Congress, Henry Clay in particular, used to contend that it was a concurrent power, possessed by the president and Congress alike, the latter deriving its authority from its control over foreign trade and appropriations. In 1818, Speaker Clay sponsored in the House of Representatives an amendment to an appropriations bill to spend a sum of money "for one year's salary and an outfit to a minister" to the South American provinces that had broken free from Spain. It was defeated; but in 1821 he tackled the problem again, this time employing a resolution which announced that the House would support the president whenever he deemed it expedient to recognize the provinces. When he was good and ready in 1822, President Monroe extended recognition.

Years later, when in 1896–97 the Congress considered a resolution purporting to recognize the independence of Cuba, then under the heel of Spanish domination, some senators advanced the argument that the right to grant recognition belonged exclusively to the Congress. The incident came to an end when the

Senate Foreign Relations Committee studied the subject and reported that the right belonged exclusively to the president rather than to Congress; a congressional resolution of recognition without presidential support would, the report said, "be a nullity." The long reach of executive monopoly over diplomacy cannot be matched by any weapon the Congress has been able to devise. Every recognition of a new government or state given by the United States has been granted by the chief executive, never by Congress.

During the "great debate" in 1951 over President Truman's dispatch of troops to Europe for the purpose of implementing American commitments under the NATO Pact, the Senate, in a hostile mood, formulated a resolution challenging his authority. Prominent senators, led by Senator Taft, contended that the president had no authority to send troops abroad without the approval of Congress. President Truman replied in a press conference that as commander-in-chief he could send troops anywhere he pleased. After a lengthy altercation, the Senate adopted a resolution designed to extend belated approval in this one instance but to concede nothing in principle and to warn the executive not to ignore the Congress again. The resolution stated, "It is the sense of the Senate that the President of the United States, as Commander-in-Chief of the armed forces, before taking action to send units of ground troops to Europe . . . should consult the Committee on Foreign Relations of the Senate, the Committee on Foreign Affairs of the House of Representatives." To complicate the process further, the resolution would require that assignment of troops abroad could in the future be made only after the Joint Chiefs of Staff certified to the secretary of defense that the assignment was necessary to American security. Subsequent presidents have ignored the cumbersome procedure prescribed in the resolution—in Vietnam, in the Dominican Republic, and elsewhere.

Experience has shown that congressional resolutions to curb

114

the president's diplomatic and military powers are impotent. They can embarrass and weaken the president in his conduct of foreign affairs, but unless he is willing to surrender to the pressure, they cannot in themselves alter policy.

The impatience of Congress with the president's control of foreign relations has impelled it to attack his authority to make executive agreements. To the Senate in particular, such agreements have appeared as a tricky method for avoiding its advise-and-consent procedure. To the president, they offer, in addition to an intended evasion of the Senate, other advantages: they can be concluded quickly, unlike a treaty, which normally requires months or even years of time in the Senate; and they can provide a shield of secrecy in delicate security situations where an enemy might benefit from a disclosure of the contents of a treaty.

Once the Senate has become aware that an agreement without approval by the Senate or the Congress is in the offing, it can be counted upon to protest. In 1943 when Secretary Hull indicated that he was about to commit the United States to participation in the United Nations Relief and Rehabilitation Administration by means of a simple agreement instead of a treaty, several members of the Senate Foreign Relations Committee—Thomas Connally, Arthur Vandenberg, Elbert Thomas, and Robert LaFollette, Jr.—challenged him in person. They were suspicious that if the Senate were evaded here, it might be later in the peace settlement ahead. The upshot was a compromise: the senators would abandon their demand for a treaty if the secretary would submit the agreement to approval by a majority of both houses of Congress in a joint resolution.

What many members of the Senate would like and have sought is to curb the president's power to make executive agreements. This was one of the purposes of Senator Bricker's proposals, which in 1951–54 were discussed both in the Congress and in the country and appeared for a time to have a chance of adoption as an amendment to the Constitution. One article of the proposals stipulated that "the Congress shall have power to regulate all executive and other agreements with any foreign power or international organization." The administration opposed the Bricker proposals as injurious to its conduct of foreign relations, and in time the project fell by the wayside.

Recently Senator Fulbright has taken up the cause of destroying the president's agreement-making power. On July 31, 1967, he submitted to the Senate a proposed resolution to the effect that

> Whereas accurate definition of the term national commitment in recent years has become obscured: Therefore, be it resolved that it is the sense of the Senate that a national commitment by the United States to a foreign power necessarily and exclusively results from affirmative action taken by the executive and legislative branches of the United States government through means of a treaty, convention, or other legislative instrumentality specifically intended to give effect to such a commitment.

Explaining his concern, the senator cited a statement by Vice-President Humphrey on April 19, 1966, that at the Honolulu Conference the previous February there had been concluded "a pledge to ourselves and to posterity to defeat aggression, to defeat social injustice, to build viable, free political institutions and achieve peace" in Vietnam. Senator Fulbright was alarmed, too, by a statement from Secretary of State Rusk that "bilateral assistance agreements justified American military efforts in Vietnam."

This so-called National Commitment Resolution rested in the Senate for two years. In June, 1969, it was revised to be more specific about what constitutes a "commitment" and to indicate in particular how a commitment might be related to the use of the armed forces in behalf of other nations. In its revised form

116

the Senate adopted it by a vote of seventy to sixteen. Following are its provisions:

> Whereas accurate definition of the term "national commitment" in recent years has become obscured: Now, therefore, be it
>
> Resolved, that a national commitment for the purpose of this resolution means the use of the armed forces on foreign territory, or a promise to assist a foreign country, government, or people by the use of the armed forces or financial resources of the United States, either immediately or upon the happening of certain events, and
>
> That it is the sense of the Senate that a national commitment by the United States results only from affirmative action taken by the legislative and executive branches of the United States government by means of a treaty, statute, or concurrent resolution of both houses of Congress specifically providing for such commitment.

The resolution had encountered only one dissenting voice in the Foreign Relations Committee—that of Senator Gale McGee. In his minority report he explained its faults as he saw them:

> As a great power, American actions cause reverberations all around the globe and must, therefore, be carefully weighed and delicately executed. Not infrequently they must be carried out swiftly. The decision-making process may be reduced by events to a matter of a single day, or even hours. On more than one occasion the time allotted by crisis incidents to those who must make the decisions has been less than the time it would take to assemble a quorum of the Congress.
>
> Possibly an even greater factor which presses for increasing the power of the president in making foreign policy in recent decades has been the advent of the nuclear age. We live in a time when 15 minutes could spell the difference between life and death for millions of people—possibly even for life itself on earth. . . .
>
> The President alone under the Constitution has authority to recognize foreign governments and to enter into commitments which

117

implement that recognition. In the conduct of the foreign relations of the United States, the President necessarily must have the power to make many commitments to foreign governments. . . .

At best, the Senate resolution has only the capabilities of mischief-making with the responsibilities of the president of the United States in foreign affairs, particularly in times like the present.

Senator Mike Mansfield called the allegation that the resolution would tie the hands of the president in foreign affairs "a lot of balderdash." In a sense he was right, for the resolution will probably be ignored by present and future presidents as both unconstitutional and unworkable in the fast-moving world of diplomacy. The president's powers in foreign affairs are derived from the Constitution and can hardly be altered by a Senate resolution. In 1912 a rider was added to an appropriations bill forbidding the president to extend or accept an invitation to an international conference without the consent of Congress; following the practice of their predecessors, subsequent presidents have sought approval only when circumstances permitted and they saw fit to do so, treating the law as an infringement on their constitutional authority in diplomacy. At most, the effect of the resolution will be to notify the president that the Senate believes itself neglected in foreign affairs. Senator Vance Hartke said that the resolution is "an invitation to the executive to reconsider its excesses." If the president agrees that he has committed excesses, he may accept the invitation.

The investigative power possessed by both the Senate and the House is another legislative weapon in foreign affairs and one which has had increasing use. Theoretically its purpose is to enable the Congress to obtain information to serve as a basis for legislation, but actually it is almost certain to be inspired by political motives—to penetrate the secrecy surrounding a situation, to find a scapegoat, to prepare for a political campaign, or to gain personal publicity. Incidentally, it is also a check on the chief executive, a threat against wrongdoing and avoidable mistakes, and a reason for generous consultation by him with legislative leaders. Some investigations have attracted wide public interest both at home and abroad: the munitions investigation by the Nye Committee in 1934, the inquiry into the recall of General MacArthur by President Truman in 1951, and the McCarthy investigations of loyalty in the State Department and the foreign service in the early 1950s.

The Congress constantly strives to be a stronger force in the control of foreign relations. It would at least place its hand on the steering wheel alongside that of the president, and at times it appears ambitious to be both the lone pilot and the navigator. This urge is most apparent in the Senate, where the advise-and-consent power in treaty making is often dubiously interpreted by some members as implying the right to advise and consent in all policy decisions.

The total volume of decision making required in foreign affairs has increased many times for the United States in the decades since World War I as a result of the continuing revolution in international relationships—more nations, more urgent economic and social problems, more destructive weapons of war, more ideologically inspired aggressions, and more need for American leadership. The inevitable consequence has been a deep absorption with international problems throughout the entire government, and especially in the office of the chief executive. When he was in the Senate, Hubert Humphrey wrote, "If the Senate's responsibilities have increased ten-fold, the international responsibilities of the Executive Branch have increased a hundred-fold." As brought out earlier, power has drifted into the president's office to such a great extent because it is there that facilities for the management of foreign relations are most effectual. Inevitable as this development has been, it has aroused fear and resentment in the hearts of many Americans, and in the Congress it has quickened the ever latent urge for war on the chief executive.

The leader in the recent controversy between the Senate and the president has been Senator Fulbright, chairman of the Foreign Relations Committee. In 1967 he regretted that the authority of the Congress in foreign policy had been steadily eroding since 1940. This erosion he attributed to the "era of crises in which urgent decisions have been required . . . of a kind that the Congress is ill-equipped to make with what has been thought to be the requisite speed." He believed that the executive branch often exaggerated the need for quick action and therefore had made mistakes that "might have been avoided by greater deliberation" within the Senate. He observed a greater uneasiness in the Senate over the extent of executive power and an increased readiness to challenge decisions that a few years ago would have gone unchallenged and "to distinguish between real emergencies and situations which, for reasons of executive convenience, are only said to be emergencies." The senator noted two areas of power in foreign affairs: "the shaping of foreign policy," its direction and purpose, and the "day-to-day conduct of foreign policy." The first is the area, so he thought, in which the Congress should be more active. The president, he contended, had facilitated the erosion of the power of Congress by obtaining in advance resolutions approving actions he might later wish to take, as in 1955 when the Congress, in the Formosa Resolution, gave him the right to defend not only Formosa and the Pescadores but also "related positions and territories [the off-shore islands of Quemoy and Matsu]."

In the hearings of the Senate Foreign Relations Committee from 1966 to 1970 the senator and some of his colleagues challenged executive decisions in Vietnam and elsewhere in an apparent effort to reclaim authority they believed to be properly lodged in the Senate or in Congress. Actually the powers which senators and representatives have been seeking are not powers they have had and lost. Never have they possessed under the Constitution or established in practice a right to approve or veto executive agreements or "commitments"; it has always been assumed that the Constitution's reference to "agreements" as well as to "treaties" empowered the president to make the former as well as to negotiate the latter. Instead of reclaiming its own eroded power, the Senate appears intent on contributing to the erosion of powers always exercised by the president.

A legislative body is necessarily limited in its capacity to deal with foreign affairs. The Revolutionary fathers discovered this in their experience under the Articles of Confederation, from 1777 to 1789. The Congress, the only organ created under the Articles, conducted foreign affairs at first through a Committee of Foreign Affairs which John Jay, in a letter from his diplomatic post in Madrid in 1780, condemned as ineffective; later, it provided for a secretary of foreign affairs, but, as the incumbent, Robert Livingston, complained, the Congress interfered with his operations, defining policies in resolutions and even dealing directly with foreign governments, so that there was no center of operations. This disappointing experience was one reason why the Constitutional Convention decided on strong executive powers in foreign affairs.

A body as large as the Congress, or even the Senate alone, cannot organize itself for competence in policy making. For one thing, its operations are scattered among committees and subcommittees in both houses, and each concerns itself with only a small segment of the whole area of foreign affairs. There is nobody in Congress who has an overall perspective in foreign policy. No unifying authority exists anywhere in Congress. As R. C. Snyder and E. A. Furmis, Jr., have noted in *American Foreign Policy* (1954), "One committee grants aid to Europe in a way calculated to provide goods at the lowest price, but another insists that half of all shipments be made in American ships, whose freight rates are higher."

President Washington in 1789 had a disillusioning altercation over foreign affairs with the Senate. On August 22 he went to that body in person to consult with it on a proposed treaty with the southern Indians, in accordance with the advise-and-consent procedure of the new Constitution. At that time there were only twenty-six members of the Senate, few enough so that it could have acted in an advisory capacity as originally expected. He hoped for a constructive discussion of his project, but instead the Senate insisted on referring it to a committee. This defeated the president's purpose and he left the Senate chamber angry, saying he would "be damned" if he ever again went to the Senate. Legislative bodies, which invariably work through committees, are hardly fitted for the heavy role in policy making which the Congress seeks.

Reference has been made to the relevancy of information to the policy-making process and to the president's strength in this respect. The so-called information revolution has never benefited the Congress as much as the chief executive, although congressional resources have improved. The president is free to turn over to Congress or its leaders whatever intelligence he wishes to pass on, and in fact he does give them much, although less than they would like. Often in resolutions one or both houses request information, but it is within the president's discretion to comply or not, as the public interest requires. While working on the London Treaty on naval armaments in 1930, the Senate requested from President Hoover information relating to its negotiation and was refused. The precedent for this refusal had been established by President Washington, who rejected the request of the House of Representatives for papers bearing on the negotiation of the Jay Treaty. For the most part, presidents have been reasonably generous in acceding to congressional requests when security considerations or the interests and wishes of other states did not prevent it.

The Senate and House derive useful information from their committee hearings at which the knowledge and opinions of persons with different backgrounds and capability, including government officials and experts, testify. The committees employ staffs of specialists to aid them in their work, and members also benefit from the services of the Legislative Reference Bureau. Complaints have been common that the committee staffs are wholly inadequate. The main deficiency of the committees in their sources of information is, however, their inability to tap as a matter of right the huge supply of intelligence lodged in the office of the chief executive, intelligence relating to current issues, without which a consideration of alternate courses of action and decision making must be handicapped.

Senators and representatives justify their junkets abroad on the ground that they need a first-hand acquaintance with the people and governments involved in issues before them. They carry on personal correspondence with leaders abroad to inform themselves, and in some instances they subscribe to foreign journals and newspapers. Members of Congress have often said that these efforts of their own do in fact pay off; a visit of a few weeks in the Middle East, a trip to Vietnam, or a letter from a member of the British House of Commons can be helpful, but again, these sources are no substitute for the fund of intelligence possessed by the chief executive. Early in 1939, Senator Borah unwittingly disclosed the fallibility of such intelligence sources when he confidently asserted that he had reliable information direct from Europe to the effect that there would be no war during the year. As a senator, Mr. Humphrey bemoaned the plight of Congress in regard to intelligence, its lack of "competent independent sources of fact and wisdom." The result, he said, is that, "faced with an impressive case by the Administration and unarmed with counter facts and arguments, even a conscientious Senator sometimes vacillates between giving a grudging consent and opposing for the sake of opposing." This defect of Congress in foreign affairs is congenital; to date no preventive or cure for it has been found. It is one reason why the conduct of foreign affairs by its very nature is an executive function. It explains the inevitable tendency toward an accretion of presidential power, especially in periods of prolonged crises.

Neither the Congress as a whole nor the Senate alone has yet found itself in the foreign-policy scheme of things. Both appear completely unhappy in their present positions, determined to move out of them but unable to find a means of locomotion or a place to go. Feeling the urge to do something, they use to the utmost and with little restraint their negative powers of harassment.

The ideal relationship between the president and Congress in foreign policy, as both would enthusiastically agree, is cooperation. Both would truthfully claim that much cooperation occurs, that they continually strive for more, and that they regret their many failures to achieve it. Especially irksome to Americans and to friends abroad obliged to live with those failures is that they so often center about vital issues like Vietnam, that breakdowns in policy occur at the very point where strength and steadiness are most imperative. For the failures, each branch of the government, like a schoolboy after a fight, blames the other. There have been times when the president has been at fault, as President Wilson was in 1919, when he did not include in his peace mission to Paris any member of the Senate. More often the failures have stemmed from a refusal on Capitol Hill to recognize the inherent advantages of the executive in foreign relations and from a sense of uncertainty about how the Congress can most profitably cooperate.

What is the appropriate role of the legislative branch in policy? The criterion to be applied in distinguishing between activities in which it can constructively take part and those in which it is destructive is, of course, its competence or incompetence; it should engage itself where its competence is clear, and freely recognize the points at which the policy-making resources of the president are superior. The translation of this generalization into specific rules of conduct is the problem. The objective in view must be the most effective foreign policy attainable, not the satisfaction of any ambition for power that may reside in either the executive or the legislative branch of government. Below are guidelines for a delimitation of areas in which congressional or senatorial action is likely to produce strength as opposed to weakness in policy.

1. *Initiative in Policy*

Although the president is better equipped to initiate policy, this is not an area of action in which the Congress is impotent. The chief executive has substantial advantages: his ability to open negotiations with other nations looking toward a treaty or an agreement, his speeches to the Congress or the nation announcing intended courses of action, his requests to Congress for statutes or funds essential to set up a policy project, and his control of the armed forces. From a structural point of view, the president is one man assisted by advisers, and therefore able to construct a policy project more expeditiously and more secretly than a Congress of 535 members. In devising a course of action, he will be aided, too, by his excellent fund of pertinent information, an asset to the policy maker at many points.

The Congress has no direct means of initiating policies on its own, principally because it has no means of establishing official contacts abroad; it has no way in which it can officially speak for the United States. But it can indirectly initiate policy by suggesting a program of action to the president. This can be done by individual members of Congress in conversation with or in written communications to the chief executive, or by a resolution, concurrent or simple (House or Senate), addressed to him. The president is free either to ignore such resolutions or to follow the advice which they contain. In itself, however, a resolution cannot create a policy. Even the Magdalena Bay Resolution of 1912 could not have established a policy if the president had chosen to reject it or to ignore it in case its provisions were challenged by a foreign power. A program suggested to the executive is only a wish unless and until it can be converted into action, and this the Congress cannot do.

Some congressional resolutions have rather obviously succeeded in prodding the executive toward a policy. The Ball-Burton-Hill-Hatch Resolution adopted by the Senate in 1943 urging President Roosevelt to call a meeting of members of the United Nations for the purpose of forming a permanent postwar organization was a stimulus toward planning for the peace to come, both in and out of the government, and led ultimately to the Dumbarton Oaks Conference in 1944. A resolution of this kind serves not only to urge a policy on the president but also to convey to him by implication a pledge of support and cooperation.

2. A Check on the President

The powers of the Congress are so fundamental that, potentially at least, it could thwart the government and bring it to a standstill in foreign affairs. It could deny appropriations for diplomatic activities and thus cut off all contacts abroad; the Senate alone could do the same thing by rejecting all presidential nominees for appointments to foreign capitals and all treaties submitted to it. The Congress could refuse to maintain any or all of the armed services and thereby amputate the president's military arm in foreign relations. So drastic would such actions be that no legislative body would even consider them; like nuclear weapons, they are too terrible to be useful.

What Capitol Hill tries to do is to examine the president's

requests for money, armament, and statutes, and to weigh the merits of his treaty projects and his diplomatic nominations, in order to find out whether it should acquiesce either in whole or in part. This undertaking, which a century ago was relatively simple, has become so complicated that the two houses of Congress are now overwhelmed. The intricacies of the budget cannot be wisely analyzed with the time and information available. Passing judgment on the need for supporting legislation and on the merits of proposed treaties involves a grasp of the facts of current international politics which congressmen lack and do not have the time or resources to acquire. To make matters worse, the organization and procedure of Congress have become so outdated that an overhauling is necessary for that body to do what it might. The total result is that the Congress is inclined to go along with executive requests rather than run the risk of a fatal mistake, or to obstruct such requests just for the sake of showing that it can.

Although the Congress has been unable to give executive requests for money and supporting statutes the thorough checking and rechecking that might seem desirable, it does put them through a certain refining process which must be regarded as beneficial as far as it goes. As executive projects are filtered through the committees and subcommittees of the Senate and House, needed changes are brought to light and adopted. This process has the further advantage that executive officials, called upon to testify before congressional committees, are obliged to rethink the reasoning supporting their projects before critical audiences.

A potentially harmful result of the checking process is an undue delay caused by extended deliberations on a project requiring immediate attention. In 1826 the Senate debated so long on President Adams's proposal to send envoys to a conference at Panama that when its confirmation was finally given, the conference was nearly over and there was no point to sending them. Dilatory practices are more serious in periods of crisis. Early in 1917, when President Wilson requested Congress for authorization to arm American merchantmen for self-defense, the Senate delayed a decision by a filibuster which killed the proposal; he was able in this instance, however, to overcome the handicap by resorting to his powers as commander-in-chief and arming the ships on his own. What the Senate deprived him of was a show of unity to Germany.

3. Advice to the President

Strange as it may seem, before 1901 no secretary of state nor any of his subordinates appeared before congressional committees to testify. Secretary of State John Hay rejected a request from Francis Loomis, an official in his department, to be allowed to appear before the Senate Foreign Relations Committee; such an appearance, the secretary believed, would be "improper and undignified." But his successor, Elihu Root, better acquainted with the ways of Congress, saw the advantages of the idea and inaugurated the practice of frequent testimony before the committee which to this day is followed with benefit both to the executive branch and to the Senate. These appearances not only provide information helpful to senators in their foreign-relations work, but also afford the executive an opportunity to sound out the opinions, doubts, and fears of the legislators. While the procedure is usually regarded as one by which the executive advises the Congress, it is also one by which the Congress advises the executive.

In addition to their collective advice in resolutions, congressmen have many opportunities both individually and in groups to submit their opinions (in person or in writing) to the president, the secretary of state, or subordinate officials in the State Department. The chief executive almost as a matter of course invites the leaders of both parties in both houses to his office before initiating an important policy move. The proceedings of these meetings are not published; they are informal, and what occurs in them is for the president to prescribe. President Kennedy met congressional leaders before acting in response to Russian missiles in Cuba in 1962 and so did President Johnson before dispatching marines to the Dominican Republic in 1965. Congressmen have since complained that the president did not seek their advice on those two occasions but merely told them his plans. In such crises when time is of the essence, protracted discussions are quite obviously not to be expected. In any event, the president is free to seek advice where he chooses; except in the case of treaties and appointments, there exists no right in Congress to advise, and in those two cases the right is in the Senate alone. The practice of consulting with leaders of Congress as much as time and circumstances permit is nevertheless a constructive one.

Congressmen are likely to feel resentful and neglected when their advice is not followed. Senator Fulbright and other anti-war senators vehemently expressed their disappointment that President Johnson did not deescalate the war in Vietnam as they advised. They felt that the executive had been indifferent to the advisory role of the Senate. What senators and representatives are likely to overlook is that the president receives conflicting advice from administrative officials as well as from legislators and that he must make a choice among the options presented to him. He is the nation's official decision maker.

4. *Criticism and Dissent*

The Convention of 1787, realizing the utility of dissent both in domestic and in foreign affairs, wrote into the Constitution a guarantee to congressmen that for "any speech or debate in either House, they shall not be questioned in any other place." The First Amendment, extending free speech to all Americans, reinforced the right of senators and representatives to speak their minds freely on public issues. Able as they are, almost to a man, they could by their criticism strengthen foreign policy immeasurably. Actually, their dissent has tended to be intemperate and irresponsible, especially in the Senate and on the more momentous issues of policy.

The president and the Senate dissenters have been pitted against each other in the "great debates" within the government on policy since World War I: the League of Nations issue (1919–20), policy toward the war in Europe (1939–41), and the Vietnam war (1964–69). The debate in the country itself over the League was clearly sparked by the Senate's challenge, under the leadership of Senator Lodge, to President Wilson's peace treaties (in which the Covenant was included). The dissenters from presidential policies in the other two "great debates" appeared in the Senate and the country at about the same time. In all three instances the president and the dissident senators appealed to the people for support, the former to maintain a policy he was pursuing and the latter to break it.

As in the country, debate in the Senate over Vietnam has gone through two stages: first it was an attack on the presidential policy of preventing a Communist takeover of South Vietnam by force; later it became an effort to coerce the president into granting the enemy concessions in order to move more rapidly toward a peace settlement. The first has already been discussed in an earlier chapter. The second began with charges that the president was evading negotiations; during the early months of 1968 it took the form of a demand to stop the bombing of North Vietnam in order to entice the enemy to the peace table. Johnson held out for a time while he asked the Communists to match such a concession with one of their own. Without any formal agreement for mutual deescalation and while a rumor was circulating that the enemy had stated secretly that it would not take advantage of a bombing halt, delegates of the two belligerents began deliberations at Paris in March, 1968. Immediately the

Communists demanded the withdrawal of American troops and materiel from Vietnam before taking up substantive issues of a peace settlement. While the Communist negotiators clung to this position, impatient senators criticized the president's stand and demanded further deescalation on a unilateral basis. They were in effect pulling the rug out from under the president's diplomatic feet.

For some four or five months after President Nixon entered the White House, the dove senators dropped their feud with the chief executive in order to give him a chance to end the war. Then, when the attack was renewed, Nixon was accused of following Johnson's policies, of escalating hostilities, of supporting an evil regime in Saigon, and of intransigence in negotiations. Senator Jacob Javits set forth four principles for a peace settlement. Senator Edward Kennedy criticized American military tactics, especially the attack on Hamburger Hill. A little later on, in October, Senator Charles E. Goodell introduced a bill which would require the president to withdraw all American troops from Vietnam by December 1, 1970. Secretary of Defense Laird pointed out that such action by the Congress would undermine the negotiations at Paris, that by stalling for fourteen months the Communists would get all they had been fighting for, together with a virtual surrender by the United States. In the midst of the controversy, Senator Hugh Scott asked for a Senate moratorium of sixty days on criticism of the president's peace efforts in order to give negotiations a chance; this proposal found no support from dissident senators.

On June 5, President Nixon took up the challenge to his policies. He denounced the "new isolationists" and those who "grow weary of the weight of free world leadership." The next morning the newspapers reported the reactions of selected senators to the president's remarks. Senator Fulbright believed they were a "form of demagoguery" and an "un-American approach

131

to stifle discussions of legitimate problems." In October the president several times explained that successful negotiations in Paris depended upon unity at home, and he pleaded for cooperation.

To negotiate a peace settlement without conceding everything to the enemy in the midst of the expressed impatience of leading senators (and prominent leaders throughout the country) was obviously not possible. The advantages which American impatience and dissent were providing the enemy came out on June 19, when Ambassador Lau reminded American Ambassador Walsh (temporarily substituting for Ambassador Lodge) of the demands in the United States for a deescalation of hostilities and for bringing the troops home. A few senators (with other dissenters) had knocked into a cocked hat Walsh's argument earlier that same day for a mutual withdrawal of troops. On July 1, Vice-President Agnew noted the plethora of experts on Vietnam in the country and reminded them that their public statements were impeding negotiations for peace. At the same time Senator Carl Curtis of Nebraska urged his colleagues to use self-restraint in their criticism of presidential policies in order to give American negotiators in Paris a chance.

Attacks in the Senate on presidential policies have a way of centering in the Foreign Relations Committee under the leadership of its chairman. Many chairmen have thought of themselves primarily as spokesmen for the administration, to gain support for executive policies and, where appropriate, guide them to adoption by the Senate; such men were William Stone (1914–18), Gilbert Hitchcock (1918–19), and Thomas Connally (1949–53). Others, men like Charles Sumner (1861–71), William Borah (1924–33), and J. William Fulbright (1959–), have looked upon themselves and their committee as an independent part of the policy-making machine, free to emasculate executive policies and to enunciate their own. The latter group, often sharing the headlines with the president, throw policy into confusion.

132

The objection that must be raised to the conduct of senators and, to a lesser degree, representatives, in foreign policy is not that they dissent; rather it is to the manner of their dissent. Regardless of the importance of the issue, their dissent is expressed in full view of the foreign governments with whom our own government is dealing; almost invariably it is made in an atmosphere of emotionalism and hostility; it is pointed toward the destruction of a policy with little in the way of constructive proposals; and it lacks the kind of restraint that a viable democracy requires. Senators Mansfield, Fulbright, and others have urged "dialogues" on policy as essential to democracy, and indeed they are. The problem is not to silence dialogues but to make them productive.

Everyone would agree that the objective of congressional debate and dissent is a strong foreign policy calculated to serve the nation's interests. Agreement would also be forthcoming on the proposition that dissent can take on forms or attributes harmful to policy. Senators would probably admit, too, that although they are better equipped than the general public with resources for deliberation on policy, they are less well supplied than the chief executive. However much they may assail the president and his policies, senators would very likely go so far as to rate his character, motives, and patriotism quite as high as their own. These facts suggest much the same guidelines for congressional debate as those suggested earlier for the general public, guidelines which could make dissent purposeful and constructive, as well as democratic.

As in the general public, debate in Congress should be expected to show less restraint on policy proposals submitted by the president than on policy decisions already taken by him. The all-out debate in the Senate on the antiballistic missile project advanced by President Nixon (which required legislative authorization) was necessary; the only objection that could be raised to it would be to its revelation in figures of the American stockpile of nuclear weapons and our understanding in figures of Russian power. The heated debate over the American presence in Vietnam after the president had decided for it and the Congress had acquiesced in its Gulf of Tonkin Resolution must appear, to the contrary, not only as a destructive crusade but also as an example of serious democratic blundering in foreign policy. There are foreign policies, such as the Peace Corps program, which can be reconsidered after they have been adopted and given force, without any considerable jeopardy to the nation. But when open attacks are made on a security policy of such proportions as to call for the deployment of troops, democratic processes are out of balance.

In the Vietnam situation, and in any situation where security interests are deemed by the executive to be at stake, there are better methods of dissent open to senators and representatives than a public attack intended to rally the people in opposition. Congressmen are always free to voice their dissent privately to the president, either orally or in writing; and their opportunities for an interview with him are excellent, far better than those of other citizens. Once dissent has been registered with the official responsible for policy, the better part of wisdom for the dissenter would be to reason that he has had his day in court and will accept the subsequent ruling of that official. That this democracy allows a member of Congress who has lost in his private case against presidential policy to make a public issue of his rebuff, or that it permits the Senate Foreign Relations Committee to televise hearings designed to stir up public support against the executive, does not imply that such actions are wise or constructive. What is implied is that democracy grants rights and privileges to congressmen as well as to other citizens, the exercise of which calls for conscientious restraint. Failure to recognize this fact suggests a lack of political maturity.

9. Presidential Leadership

AMERICAN DEMOCRACY is on a blundering course in foreign policy making, today its most crucial job. Yet it remains complacent, as though by some special dispensation it were destined to go on forever. The policy fiasco in Vietnam is regarded as the normal functioning of democracy, not as a warning of more serious catastrophies ahead. The policy-making processes of the United States are out of balance both within the government and between the government and the people. They have fallen prey to democracy's twin temptations: to overestimate the ability of the people, and to distrust superior knowledge and skill.

Sobering as the experience of the United States has been, not only recently in Vietnam, but elsewhere over the last half century, to conclude that democracy's foreign policy must be self-defeating would be hasty. Were this democracy to find itself, to learn how to combine competence with popular sovereignty, it could arm itself with procedures and policies more decisive, more protective, and more righteous than any authoritarian regime could match.

The vitality of a policy depends first of all upon its contents—their devotion to the national interest as well as to the reasonable interests of others, and their practicability as means to a desired

135

end. If the policy maker were free to concentrate his thinking exclusively on interests and practicable means, his job would be simplified. But as a politician, he must listen to the opinions of others whose analyses disagree with his own, and perhaps devise a compromise policy. Even in a dictatorship like the Soviet Union there are contrary opinions to conciliate, but the conciliating process is relatively simple, for it involves only a few men at the top rather than the general public and an independent legislature. In a democracy, the job of the policy maker as a compromiser depends on the kind of public and legislative body he must consider in his thinking; his problem will always be more complicated than that of a dictator, but also less open to evil designs. In the new democracy of America, the policy maker has to deal with the toughest public and the most intractable legislative body (the Senate) to be found anywhere. The president must concern himself primarily with a policy that he can get by with in the country and only secondarily with one suited to the nation's interests. And the more he must tailor his policies to the exigencies of domestic politics, the less likely he is to come up with winners.

Here is another way in which the procedures for domestic policy making are not suited to foreign policy. The compromise of diverse opinions in domestic legislation—the opinions of farmers, labor, business, blacks, whites, Catholics, and Protestants—makes for harmony by dividing the pie so that everyone gets a slice. But a foreign policy made primarily to compromise diverse points of view and produce harmony at home will rarely be equipped for its mission abroad; acceptable internally, it risks failure externally. A policy reduced to the least common denominator of national thinking is also reduced in vitality.

The element of compromise in the Vietnam policy of President Johnson is a case in point. It was hawkish in that over five hundred thousand troops were deployed, but it was dovish in that no American ground forces were allowed in North Vietnam or Cambodia, aerial bombing of the enemy's most vulnerable targets was forbidden, and no blockade from the sea was allowed. As a compromise policy it was a failure, and as it turned out, it did not even allay the unrest at home. The new democracy, in which the people and the Senate contend with and intimidate the executive, dangerously accentuates the element of compromise always in some degree present. Halfway policies in an era of crisis can be fatal.

Once the substance of a policy has been fixed, its effectiveness depends on the circumstances surrounding its enunciation and maintenance. Here again the contest of the president with the people and the Senate saps the vitality out of American policy. For one thing, it slows up policy making as the president holds off action, hopefully awaiting a consensus to form. Where a treaty is involved in policy, the Senate likes to delay and see which way the wind will blow, always for several months at least and sometimes for a year or two. The president is constitutionally capable of moving fast in crises and sometimes has, as did President Johnson in the Dominican Republic in 1965, but he knows that what he regards as a crisis will not necessarily be one in the opinion of the people or the Senate. One of Senator Fulbright's complaints has been that the chief executive, President Johnson in particular, followed too liberal an interpretation of "emergency" in order to justify quick action and disregard of the Senate. The president's dilemma is to avoid problems or delay action until he feels able to count on support, or to act expeditiously and be denounced for seeing an emergency where none existed. American policy tends, therefore, to be poorly timed, often "'too little and too late." It took the United States two years, from 1939 to 1941, to find a policy toward the war in Europe, and when the decision came it was made, not by us, but by the Japanese.

A devitalizing ambiguity and uncertainty surround the American process of policy making; long delay, together with constant challenges to executive action, creates doubt about what American policy really is. In 1953, Clement Attlee, then leader of the British Labor party and a man experienced in dealing with the United States, explained, "The Prime Minister comes to the House of Commons and states his policy. It is the policy of the government. He can, if he wishes, get a vote in support of it in the House." The situation in the United States, he said, is quite different because the president "is not master in his own house," for "power is divided between the Administration and Congress." That the word of the president of the world's strongest power cannot be taken at face value must be annoying to other governments and confusing to international affairs generally. When in 1939–41 President Roosevelt's policy announcements were followed regularly by contradictory statements from Senator Burton Wheeler, an influential spokesman for the isolationists and a member of the Senate Foreign Relations Committee, other nations had cause for bewilderment. An ambiguous policy has within it the seeds of trouble. Enemies are tempted to test it and friends to doubt that they can rely on it.

The acrimonious debates in which our policies are enunciated and given effect also vitiate policies by the publicity they give to facts, problems, and possible plans that might better be kept secret. Politicians and people shout from the housetops our doubts, fears, and limitations. We put ourselves in the position of a football team that would be so foolish as to attach a loudspeaker to its huddle and broadcast to the opposition the next play, the ball carrier, and the players who will run the interference. We tell the Russians and Chinese that we are afraid of them and will modify our policies accordingly. We tell the Russians what our government believes it knows about their nuclear capability. We inform the Communists in Vietnam that we seek a mutual withdrawal of troops but if that is not possible, we may withdraw troops unilaterally, as in fact we did.

That all democracies face a tough problem in foreign policy making has already been sufficiently emphasized; as policy corruption by evil-minded men is the common malady of authoritarian regimes, so policy devitalization is the inherent affliction of democracies. What must be pointed out once more is that the United States faces more than the ordinary handicaps that other democracies encounter. No other nation has so demanding a people. No other nation has a Senate so determined to diminish the size of the presidency and to heighten its own. The president, the people, and the Senate make up a triangle of contention or impasse that must be broken if the nation is to find a secure peace.

The thesis of this volume is that although the people and the Senate have important contributions to make, strength in policy depends in conceding to the president a central position. Foreign policy making is by its very nature an executive function, as lawmaking (in democracies) is essentially the work of a representative parliamentary body. This does not preclude the legislature's exercise of certain necessary functions in foreign affairs nor the executive's performance of a role in legislation; but it does mean that the acknowledged decision maker in the former should be the president and in the latter the Congress. It brings out in a slightly different context, the point that American democracy can thrive in foreign relations only if the people and the Senate stay within their limitations and concede to the chief executive his rightful position.

Significance must once again be ascribed to the inevitable way that in war and in the prolonged period of crises known as the cold war the authority of the presidency expands. It is democracy's effort to meet an emergency with competence. It is democracy's way of getting the shot of adrenalin it requires for a fight. Most important, it is an admission of the foreign-policy-making advantages of the executive, of his unique position as a

Index

147

INDEX

Senate Foreign Relations Committee: appointments, 109; attacks on executive, 120–121, 132–133; hearings, 94, 123; National Commitment Resolution (1969), 117; report on recognition (1897), 113–114; staff of specialists, 65; televised hearings, 10, 94–95

Separation-of-powers system, 104–119, 124–134, 136

Seward, Secretary of State William, 52

Shotwell, James, 22

Snyder, R. C. and Furniss, E. A., Jr., 121–122

Sorensen, Theodore, 50

Stark, R., and Glock, C., 97

Stennis, Sen. John, 140

Stevenson, Adlai, 66

Sumner, Charles, 36, 132

Taft, Sen. Robert, 30, 113, 114

Television, 99–100

Tocqueville, Alexis de, 7, 50

Treaty making, 19–21, 108–109

Truman, Pres. Harry, 30, 47, 50, 66, 74, 90, 106, 114, 119, 142, 144

United Nations, 30, 106, 126

United States v Curtiss-Wright (1936), 105

Vietnam policy of U.S.: attacks on, 10, 14, 31–38, 130–131; bombing, 35, 130; ethics, 45; in recent elections, 74–82; merits, 11, 136–137; negotiations, 34, 90–92, 131–132; news media, 99–100; policy objectives, 62; Senate dissent, 130–131

Warburg, J. P., 72

Warren, Sidney, 141

Washington, Pres. George, 12–14, 40, 100, 110, 122

Webster, Daniel, 112

Wheeler, Sen. Burton K., 138

Wilson, Pres. Woodrow, 17, 20, 23, 47, 52, 81, 106, 109, 124, 128, 130

World Council of Churches, 35

World Court issue, 20–21, 109, 140

World War I, 10, 17–18, 23, 41, 43, 88

World War II, 10, 25–27, 29, 107

XYZ affair, 14

Yalta Agreement (1945), 94, 106